BRITISH TOPOGRAPHICAL SERIES

BEYOND THE GREAT GLEN

BRITISH TOPOGRAPHICAL SERIES

in preparation

Bodmin Moor
The Chilterns
Fenland Country

BEYOND THE GREAT GLEN

by JAMES R. NICOLSON

DAVID & CHARLES

NEWTON ABBOT LONDON

NORTH POMFRET (VT) VANCOUVER

ISBN 0 7153 6778 1

Set in 11 on 13pt Baskerville and printed in
Great Britain by Latimer Trend & Company
Ltd Plymouth for David & Charles (Holdings)
Limited   South Devon House   Newton Abbot
Devon

Published in the United States of America by
David & Charles Inc North Pomfret Vermont
05053 USA

Published in Canada by Douglas David &
Charles Limited   3645 McKechnie Drive
West Vancouver   BC

To Eileen and Margaret

CONTENTS

LIST OF ILLUSTRATIONS

LIST OF ILLUSTRATIONS

INTRODUCTION

THE Scottish Highlands are a huge tract of land covering half of Scotland and one-sixth of Britain, but although many are familiar with the southern Highlands, the countryside of Loch Lomond and the Trossachs, for many the Highlands end at Inverness. There is, however, another, wilder part of the Highlands—a land of mountains and valleys, of moor and forest, of shining lochs and sparkling rivers stretching north and west out into the Atlantic Ocean. It is with this northern half of the Highlands that these pages are concerned— the land beyond the Great Glen.

The Great Glen, Glen Mor in Gaelic, is aptly named: it runs in a north-east to south-west direction as a massive gash in the earth's crust, the result of earth movements millions of years ago. The line of lochs and the Caledonian canal which threads them, like beads on a necklace, make the area to the north and west effectively an island. The region shows great variation in scenery and climate but it is an easily defined unit with a troubled history and economic problems to which a solution has yet to be found.

To the east the region is bounded by the Moray Firth, a deep wedge of the North Sea terminating in three subsidiary inlets, namely the Dornoch Firth, the Beauly Firth and the Cromarty Firth. The latter is one of the best deep water harbours in the north of Scotland. The Atlantic coast is bathed by the warming water of the North Atlantic Drift and is sheltered by the myriad islands of the Hebrides, but along the north coast joining Atlantic Ocean and North Sea runs the Pentland

Firth whose tidal streams are a grave hazard to the ships of many nationalities that use this busy route.

Before the reorganisation of local government in 1974, the northern Highlands included a small part of Argyll, a large part of Inverness, most of Ross and Cromarty and the complete counties of Sutherland and Caithness. These were the names given by the Gaelic-speaking people or by the Norse settlers of a thousand years ago, but the entire area is now in the Highland region with the former counties rearranged into districts and two new ones created at Lochaber and Lochalsh.

Almost the whole of the northern Highlands is rugged and mountainous with many peaks over 3,000ft high. In this type of country every scrap of level land is vital and has to be utilised so that crofting, a special kind of small-scale farming, is the rule. There are exceptions: most of Caithness is flat and in parts of Easter Ross there are large areas of well tended farmland as fertile as that of the Lothians.

Communications are difficult but this was still more marked in the past. Penetration from the south was virtually impossible as successive English and Scottish Lowland kings and even the resourceful Oliver Cromwell were forced to realise. Sea-borne expeditions were more successful and influences rooted in Ireland and Norway made more headway for a time. For centuries the northern Highlands remained 'a country within a country'.

This is still the empty quarter of Scotland—a region of over 4 million acres yet supporting only 140,000 people. The need for development is occupying the minds of the planners and developers of today yet the very emptiness and scope for leisure activities is the great attraction of the Highlands in an over-crowded Britain. Where else in Britain can one find nature unspoiled by man—secluded beaches of clean, yellow sand that give way inland to carpets of wild flowers; and jagged mountain peaks that harbour rare Alpine plants and provide sanctuary for some of Britain's rarest animals? Even in the towns and villages life still knows a pace of peace and tranquillity that much of Britain has forgotten.

CLIMATE

The climate of the northern Highlands is as varied as its topography with a wide range of micro-climates varying from mild oceanic conditions on the west coast to sub-arctic conditions on the mountain tops. The most noticeable feature is the warming influence of the sea, for in spite of the high latitude temperatures along the coasts are remarkably mild. January temperatures in north-west Scotland are similar to those of south-east England. The average number of days per year when snow lies on the ground ranges from over 100 in places in the mountains to between 10 and 30 in Caithness and only 5 along the west coast. Mild winters with few frosts make it possible to grow sub-tropical plants in the famous gardens at Inverewe, and these attract over 100,000 visitors each year.

High rainfall is a feature of most of this area. The prevailing south-westerly air stream is moist as it leaves the sea and dumps its water-load on the western side of the Highlands as it rises to cross the mountains. The rainfall averages 100 to 150in a year over a wide area from Kyle of Lochalsh almost to Fort William. One of the wettest parts of Britain is Glen Garry with over 200in a year, but around the Moray Firth in the shelter of the mountains, the climate is entirely different with a low annual rainfall of around 25in. High rainfall, exploited in hydro-electric schemes, has been turned into one of the greatest economic assets of the Highlands.

Wind speeds are high along the west and north coasts and on high ground. South-westerlies are usual although westerly winds are common in April and at the end of the year, while the south-easterlies of spring are cold, blowing off the snow-capped central Highlands. Wick is less sheltered than either Inverness or Fort William but surprisingly the frequency of days with

	Jan	Feb	March	April	May	June	July	Aug	Sept	Oct	Nov	Dec	Total
WICK													
Sunshine (hours) 1931–60	44	72	111	152	175	165	147	135	120	87	52	34	1,294
Temperature (° C) 1931–60	3·3	3·6	4·7	6·3	8·4	10·8	12·8	12·7	11·4	9·0	6·4	4·6	
Rainfall (inches) 1916–50	2·93	2·00	1·81	2·03	1·81	2·04	2·57	2·63	2·90	3·12	3·16	2·97	29·97
Wind speed (mph) (Airport, 1968–70)	16·7	14·7	17·1	14·5	13·5	10·9	11·3	10·6	12·9	14·7	15·3	15·2	
INVERNESS													
Sunshine (hours) 1931–60	42	68	107	137	174	171	140	130	121	89	47	30	1,256
Temperature (° C) 1931–60	3·2	3·8	5·2	7·8	10·4	13·1	14·7	14·5	12·6	9·3	6·2	3·9	
Rainfall (inches) 1916–50	2·49	1·74	1·38	1·64	1·95	1·79	2·68	2·83	2·42	2·67	2·29	2·10	25·98
Wind speed (mph) (Dalcross, 1968–70)	10·0	10·6	11·9	10·6	10·0	7·9	9·8	7·6	9·2	10·8	10·1	9·9	
FORT WILLIAM													
Sunshine (hours) 1931–60	15	46	90	117	177	153	113	117	87	57	23	7	1,002*
Temperature (° C) 1931–60	3·0	3·5	5·7	7·7	10·7	12·9	14·1	14·2	12·2	9·5	6·1	4·3	
Rainfall (inches) 1916–50	9·84	7·09	5·00	4·75	3·94	4·45	5·27	5·95	6·95	9·13	7·74	8·57	78·68
Wind speed (mph) (Corpach 1968–70)	10·8	9·8	12·1	10·0	11·2	10·5	11·6	8·9	10·1	12·8	11·3	8·9	

* N.B.—At Fort William the sunshine record is curtailed by high ground to the south.

Weather statistics for Wick, Inverness and Fort William

strong gusts is greater at Fort William than at Wick, especially in summer and autumn. Degree of shelter has an important bearing on local climate. Bare exposed headlands such as Cape Wrath and Ardnamurchan Point defy the Atlantic breakers that beat below the cliffs; but long sheltered inlets like Loch Carron, and Loch Linnhe allow the forest to extend almost to the edge of the sea. Where there is shelter from the wind primroses may bloom in the depth of winter, in the lee of a boulder or among dead ferns, but in exposed situations the force of the wind can damage tall plants and the leaves of trees suffer excessive evaporation. Plockton, on a sheltered inlet of Loch Carron, has a sub-tropical appearance with palm trees growing in the cottage gardens but the wind-swept plains of Caithness have few forests and sycamores growing behind garden walls are stunted by the wind.

Humidity is generally as high as 75 to 80 per cent along the west and north coasts—a feature that brings out hordes of midges in the still summer evenings. Thunderstorms are infrequent, ranging from about four days a year in Caithness to about six at Fort William but the rate increases rapidly southwards to give about fifteen days a year in London. Thunderstorms can be impressive, however; the mountain known as An Teallach or The Forge is supposed to have been given its name on account of the lightning flickering around its summit during hailstorms in winter.

The number of sunshine hours is low averaging only between 20 and 30 per cent of those possible. There are only 30 days per year with more than 9 hours of bright sunshine compared to 60 or 70 along the south coast of England. Visibility is quite a different matter: along the Moray Firth, in Caithness and the extreme north-west of Scotland visibility is greater than $6\frac{1}{4}$ miles on more than 300 days of the year compared with only 200 to 250 along the south coast. There is little thick fog in the northern Highlands. The purity of the air is one of the attractions of Caithness and it is astonishing over how many miles the modest peaks of Morven and the Scarabens dominate the landscape.

The interior of the northern Highlands is wild and inhospitable, composed of hard unyielding rocks once scalped by glaciers and now lashed with rain and swept by high winds. One can travel many miles and see only remote sheep farms, a shepherd on the hills, a deer stalker, or a group of road maintenance men. Settlement is mainly confined to the coasts, the lower reaches of the wide straths and along the Great Glen. The land is generally poor and difficult to farm and even today, after centuries of habitation, only a mere fraction is under crops and grass and most of this lies along the eastern coastal strip. In the west and north the basic agricultural unit is the croft—a holding of 5 to 10 acres of arable land sandwiched between the sea-shore and the barren hills. The holdings are generally grouped together in townships of a dozen or more crofts that share the pasture of the hills, each crofter having a share of the sheep that graze there.

This is a region of small towns and villages but they are few and far between. Only the town of Inverness has over 30,000 inhabitants, next comes Thurso with 10,000 and Wick with 8,000, while Dingwall, the administrative centre of Ross and Cromarty, has little more than 4,000. Each of these settlements is of greater relative importance to its surrounding area than an English village of similar size. Many of them, such as Cromarty and Dingwall, are delightful little burghs with charters going back to the thirteenth century and with a romance and history in their yellow sandstone buildings.

Crofting

Crofting is a form of subsistence agriculture peculiar to the Highlands and islands of Scotland. The patches of arable land produce oats, barley and potatoes for human consumption and winter fodder for livestock; the hills provide summer grazing for sheep and cattle, and can still produce peat for fuel; the beaches yield seaweed for manure and shellfish; the sea produces fish for sale, for eating fresh and for salting as a winter standby. Crofting is of great historical and present consequence over most of the northern Highlands; but it is far more than just an industry—it is a way of life.

West from Thurso and then on down the west coast, the great dome of the atomic energy establishment at Dounreay is the last symbol of industrialisation the visitor sees until he reaches the paper mill of Corpach near Fort William. As he leaves the plain of Caithness he enters typical crofting territory with such attractive coastal settlements as Portskerra, Bettyhill, Tongue and Durness, while inland crofts are worked in the re-settled valleys of Strathnaver and Strath Halladale and around Knockan and Elphin in the limestone areas of Sutherland.

Sutherland is unique in Britain—a vast territory of over $1\frac{1}{4}$ million acres with only 13,000 inhabitants and most of those live in villages on the coast. The interior is really bleak and takes on an arctic appearance in winter but in summer it is a totally different world where the strong light glints on moorland lochans and the air is alive with the sound of birds.

In Sutherland all roads converge on Lairg, a delightful village and the centre of a sheep-farming area, very busy in autumn at the time of the great sheep and cattle sales. Lairg is the shopping centre for a wide district and has a first class hotel and other tourist accommodation but in spite of its obvious importance its population is little more than 300.

Along the west coast the pattern of crofting is repeated with townships set amidst the most beautiful scenery Scotland has to offer. But scenery alone cannot provide the basic needs of life and sad marks of depopulation are all too evident in abandoned crofts, although the growing importance of tourism is doing much to halt the decline.

The development of the fishing industry within the last ten years has also offered new hope to the west. There are thriving

B

ports at Kinlochbervie, Lochinver, Ullapool, Gairloch and Mallaig where fleets of modern vessels are based to fish the rich waters of the Minch. Ullapool, created by the British Fisheries Society in 1788, lies in one of the most beautiful parts of the Highlands and has also grown in importance as a holiday resort, a centre for sea-angling, water sports and pony-trekking. In 1973 it became the mainland terminal for the roll-on/roll-off ferry service to Stornoway. This was a blow to Kyle of Lochalsh, the former terminal, but Kyle remains the main crossing point for travellers to Skye. The most important port of all is Mallaig, now the main herring port in Britain.

Fishing on a much smaller scale was once important along the entire coastline. There are numerous little villages like Arnisdale and Applecross whose rows of terraced houses now take on a different role as, painted in bright colours, they offer accommodation to holiday-makers. The village of Plockton is a thriving holiday resort, a centre for yachting and the home base of the adventure schooner *Captain Scott*.

One of the areas most affected by depopulation is the extreme south-west where the parishes of Morvern and Ardgour, Arisaig and Moidart, and Ardnamurchan saw their combined population drop from 8,240 in 1851 to 2,747 in 1951. The lead mines of Strontian once offered additional income to crofters and their closure was a blow from which the region has never recovered.

The area of the Great Glen itself is exceptional in that it has maintained and even increased its population. There is better farmland in broad valleys like Glen Urquhart, Glen Moriston and Glen Garry and forestry is important, but the main reason for the increase is industrial development at Corpach and Fort William.

Communications remain a problem for the inhabitants. The narrow roads were never intended to carry the volume of traffic that they have to today and the ports of Lochinver and Mallaig are still served by single-track roads with passing places that twist around bluffs with sheer drops to the sea. In summer the drivers of the huge fish lorries have another hazard to face —the thousands of holiday-makers who seek the west coast with their cars and caravans. The narrow roads are no obstacle to tourists and add to the charm of the Highlands, while often the more difficult the road the greater the scenic reward.

Railways too are inadequate, uneconomic to operate and frequently threatened with closure; yet in summer they play an important role in the growing tourist industry since they pass through some of Scotland's best scenery. There is the famous West Highland line from Fort William, past Glenfinnan and Morar to Mallaig, and the line from Dingwall to Kyle of Lochalsh where passengers board the ferry for Skye. The north-west is poorly served, the nearest stations being Garve and Achnasheen, while for Durness and Tongue the nearest rail-head is at Lairg.

The Eastern Lowlands

The most fertile part of the northern Highlands is the coastal strip from Inverness northwards to Helmsdale. The climate is mild with a low rainfall and the sandy soil creates good farming land. This strip includes the famous Black Isle peninsula of Ross and Cromarty—a misnomer if ever there was one, especially in spring when the gorse and broom are a blaze of yellow.

Around the sheltered firths many little towns and villages bask in the sunshine. On the Cromarty Firth stands Invergordon, once an important naval base but now a rapidly growing industrial centre. At the head of the firth Dingwall is an important administrative and shopping centre while Strathpeffer, farther inland, is a tourist centre and a spa. In the Black Isle several small ports such as Cromarty, Avoch and Kessock date from the heyday of the herring fishery. Only Avoch remains a fishing village but its fishermen now operate from ports on the west coast where shoals are still prolific.

INTRODUCTION

Around the Dornoch Firth lie the attractive towns of Tain, Bonar Bridge and Dornoch itself. Dornoch has seen many changes in peace and war but its great cathedral has been preserved as a rare relic of the Middle Ages. Farther north in Sutherland are Golspie and Brora, the latter being exceptional in this part of Scotland having a large woollen mill, a distillery and the most northerly coal mine in Britain.

The plain of Caithness is quite different, separated from the rest of Scotland by bleak hills and a wide expanse of deer forest and grouse moor. It has often been called 'the Lowlands beyond the Highlands' and is an area of small farms and crofts scattered over a low, relatively fertile plateau. There are inland villages such as Watten and Halkirk but the largest settlements are situated along the coast and over half the population live in the two burghs of Wick and Thurso. Wick grew in size during the herring boom of the late nineteenth century and is still a fishing and commercial port but its harbour can only cater for vessels up to 3,000 tons. Thurso owes its recent expansion to the atomic energy establishment at Dounreay but it too maintains a fishing tradition. Nearby Scrabster is the mainland terminal for the car and passenger ferry to Orkney. South of Wick lie several small fishing villages at Lybster, Latheronwheel, Keiss, Dunbeath and Whaligoe, whose tiny harbour lies below a great sea cliff and is reached by 365 steps. All of these have declined in importance as fishing villages but have increased in importance as tourist attractions. Staxigoe, just north of Wick, was once an important sea port and saw the beginnings of the Caithness herring industry.

HISTORICAL BACKGROUND

The history of the Highlands is one of the great tragedies of Britain. Wild, inhospitable and remote, it was overtaken by developments in the rest of the country. At the beginning of the eighteenth century when the rest of Britain was settled in towns and country villages, the people of the Highlands were still divided into close-knit valley communities. They were separated from neighbouring settlements by large tracts of mountain and moorland, owing allegiance to their chief and to their clan. They spoke Gaelic, once the language of most of Scotland but surviving only in parts of the Highlands and the western islands.

The history of religion was also different here. The effects of the Reformation were slow to penetrate and many of the people remained loyal to the Stuart line of kings; this was their most serious mistake of all, at least in the eyes of the rest of Britain. In 1715 they were willing to fight when the Old Pretender arrived to claim his throne; in 1719 they were ready again but the rebellion was stopped early in its course.

The most glorious moment in the history of the Highlands, however pathetic and tragic the outcome, occurred when Prince Charles Edward Stuart raised his standard at Glenfinnan on 19 August 1745. The clans rallied to his cause and with hopes high they marched towards Edinburgh gaining supporters as they went. In November they set out for London but the English Jacobites failed them and at Derby they turned back towards Scotland. On 16 April 1746 at Culloden Moor near Inverness the army was defeated. No ship was immediately available to take the Prince to safety in France and until September 1746 he moved as a fugitive among the hills and glens of the western seaboard, a price of £30,000 on his head. No one betrayed him. Even today the visitor cannot help but visualise the lonely, romantic figure as he clambers over the same rocks, steps over the same streams and hides in the same caves as the fugitive Prince over 200 years ago.

The Prince was lucky when he escaped to France. His supporters paid dearly for their mistake, as the British government took its revenge. This was a cruel blow to Gaelic culture in the Highlands and it resulted in the end of the old clan system. In 1773 when Dr Samuel Johnson visited the area, he wrote: 'Of what they had before the late conquest of their country there remains only their language and their poverty.' Soon their language was to be eroded too.

As the bitter memories faded the British government began to examine closely the problems of the area. Roads were built and the Caledonian Canal was constructed along the Great Glen while railways soon brought the people of the northern Highlands into closer contact with the rest of the country. There were many improvements but still the region did not keep pace with the rest of Britain. While the Industrial Revolution caused the growth of large cities and the agricultural revolution transformed the face of the British countryside, the Highlanders remained crofters, existing on their few acres of land as the last real peasants in Europe.

The changes after 1745 affected agriculture most of all. The chiefs lost interest in their people and became more and more commercially minded. Like the lowland flockmasters who then began to move north, they found sheep more profitable than tenants and Blackface sheep began to invade the better hill pasture. But sheep and laird alike coveted the green valleys and the inhabitants were removed as the sheep took over. So began the terrible evictions or clearances which continued until the Crofters' Holdings Act of 1886 when the crofters were given that most fundamental of rights—security of tenure.

A mere Act of Parliament could not solve the economic ills of the Highlands. One of the most pressing problems was depopulation for the decline, once started, could not be controlled. Then sheep farming itself suffered a depression in the late nineteenth century and sheep were replaced by wild deer in many estates, their sporting value being greater than the income from sheep. The Highlands became progressively more silent as economists and lairds talked over whiskies in their London clubs about 'the Highland problem'.

About this time the empty wastes were discovered by the new English middle class, those who had made fortunes out of the

22

Industrial Revolution. They developed a taste for deer-stalking and grouse-shooting on the quiet Highland moors in a bid to escape the grime and grit of their industrial slums. Queen Victoria found her Eden at Balmoral and Sir Walter Scott's novels and poems evoked even greater interest in the region. It became fashionable for London's society to copy the Queen and build large houses which they called shooting lodges in almost every glen. The once proud Highlander became servant and ghillie through the summer, and his simple dress, the kilt and tartan, became fashionable among the wealthy. Venison and salmon graced the dining tables of the rich but they despised the crofter and regarded his Gaelic culture and language as inferior. The Highland mansions then became too costly to maintain and one by one the servants were discarded in the interest of economy.

The first half of the twentieth century saw the decay of the crofting way of life, a decline in population and an ageing populace as the young people drifted south in search of work. The wars temporarily reversed the trend.

THE REGION TODAY

The failure of the crofting system has much to do with the decline of the entire northern Highlands. For centuries crofting has been a dying industry and legislation, however essential, has merely frozen the industry in a state of near collapse. It is unfortunate that no matter how picturesque or idyllic, the white-washed cottage beside the burn, with its patches of green fields surrounded by heather hills, the croft cannot support a family by itself.

The first sign of a willingness to tackle the problem of Highland development came when the government of 1945–51 began to direct industrial development into Scotland. At the same time the North of Scotland Hydro-Electric Board began to harness water power and to take light to isolated communities.

L E W I S

Stornoway

*North
Minch*

Hand

Ba

Pt of Stoer

Lochinver

Harris

Little Minch

L Ewe

Poolewe

Gairloch Gairloch

L Maree

R O

Torridon

L Torridon

BEINN
EIGHE

Rona

S

Portree

Raasay

Applecross

Glen Carron

Toscaig

L Carron

K

Plockton Strome Ferry

Kyle of Lochalsh

Lochals

Kyleakin

L Duich

Y

Broadford

Glen Shiel

E

Arnisdale

Canna

Armadale

Sound of Sleat

Knoydart

Rum

Mallaig

N

Eigg

Arisaig

I

Muck

L Shiel

Lochaber

LE

Ardnamurchan
Point

Ardnamurchan

Coll

Morvern

Loch Linnhe

Tiree

M U L L

Iona

The

The opportunity of construction work on dams was welcome at a time of high unemployment but it was only temporary and did not solve the fundamental problem of the Highlands. The establishment of the experimental reactor at Dounreay provided a boost to Caithness and to Thurso in particular.

Most important and successful have been the efforts of the Highlands and Islands Development Board. It was set up in 1965 and in its first seven years the HIDB spent £14·2 million on agriculture and fishing and in the creation of new industries. Deliberate attempts were made to reverse depopulation by 'operation counterdrift' and by 1972 the HIDB was able to claim a halt in population decline.

Also in 1972 came the first signs of the importance of North Sea oil. The Highlands lacked coal and iron and so failed to participate in the first Industrial Revolution, but a future associated with North Sea oil cannot be avoided. The first developments occurred on the Cromarty Firth and by the end of 1972 there was actually a shortage of labour in the Dingwall–Invergordon area. The problem now is not to attract industry to the Cromarty Firth but to provide the houses, schools and roads for a greatly increased population.

All over the Highlands there are projects being planned—at Dunnet Bay in Caithness, at Loch Eriboll in Sutherland, and at several places on the west coast. It is indicative of the change in attitude that development is no longer welcomed at any price. There is a new concern for the environment as became clear at the public enquiry on proposals to build oil production platforms at Dunnet Bay in Caithness and at Drumbuie on Loch Carron.

Conservation is vital to the Highlands. Landscape and the saga of settlement in northern Britain are at risk. There is tangible proof of the peoples who have combined to make the race of Highlanders, the Norse sea rovers, the mysterious Picts and Celtic settlers from many lands. Below the peat lie the remains of Iron Age, Bronze Age, and Stone Age man. The

26

Highlands are much more than a museum; it is a living land, where stoat and otter hunt their prey and golden eagle and peregrine falcon have their last strongholds, and where old traditions survive alongside the world's newest industries.

1 THE LAND

THE fabric of the northern Highlands has undergone many changes in its long history. Even the mountains we see today are merely the roots of a former, much more massive mountain range weathered down by sun, rain, wind and the work of rivers over millions of years. In comparatively recent times glaciers spread across the land and their subsequent melting left behind a thick cover of boulder clay. The climate improved and trees began to flourish; it worsened again and an expanse of peat spread over the hillsides. Then man came upon the scene using the glacial soils to grow his crops and digging out blocks of peat for fuel. In no other part of Britain is the history of the earth more easily read.

GEOLOGY

A broad central belt of the Highlands is occupied by a bleak series of rocks known as the Moine schists. They stretch from the Firth of Lorne to the north coast and cover almost 3,500 square miles. Originally sediments of an ancient sea floor, they have been compressed, folded and uplifted and their constituent minerals have been altered by intense heat and pressure. They are Pre-Cambrian in age and date from between 800 and 1,000 million years ago.

Along the western sea-board there is a much greater variety in the rocks, more meaningful to the observer, more easily interpreted in terms of climate and geography. Again there is an ancient basement form but this time known as Lewisian

gneiss; it is even older than the Moine schists and was once part
of a vast continent stretching away to the north-west but now
hidden by younger rocks and by the Atlantic Ocean. It still
constitutes practically all of the Outer Hebrides and appears
extensively in Wester Ross and Sutherland between Glen Elg
and Loch Eriboll.

Along the southern edge of the Lewisian continent sand
accumulated and this is preserved as the Torridonian sandstone
which occurs in large pockets between Cape Wrath and the
Sound of Sleat. The greatest expanse is around Loch Torridon.
Although known to be the oldest sedimentary rocks in the
world, much can be learned of the conditions that prevailed
along the Lewisian coast of 800 million years ago. The sea was
shallow as shown by ripple marks in the sandstone but sometimes the fringing lagoons dried out and the mud cracked in
times of drought. The cracks are still visible today in the
hardened mud-stone. Of the land itself we can know little,
although the presence of wind-faceted pebbles suggests desert
conditions.

The northern continents were altered in shape; the Torridonian sandstone was raised above the sea and moulded by
erosion into hills and valleys before being submerged again to
allow sediments of Cambrian Age to accumulate. These are
found today in a belt from Loch Kishorn to Loch Eriboll and
can be divided roughly into two groups—a hard, pure white
quartzite and a great thickness of light and dark grey dolomite
and limestone. Fossils are numerous and include the remains of
strange molluscs and long-extinct sea creatures known as trilo-
bites.

About 420 million years ago the region was convulsed by
earth movements—the period known as the Caledonian
orogeny when huge mountains higher than the modern Alps
were hurled skywards and the Pre-Cambrian and Cambrian
rocks with their fossils were raised into the position they now
occupy. As part of this upheaval huge slices of the earth's crust

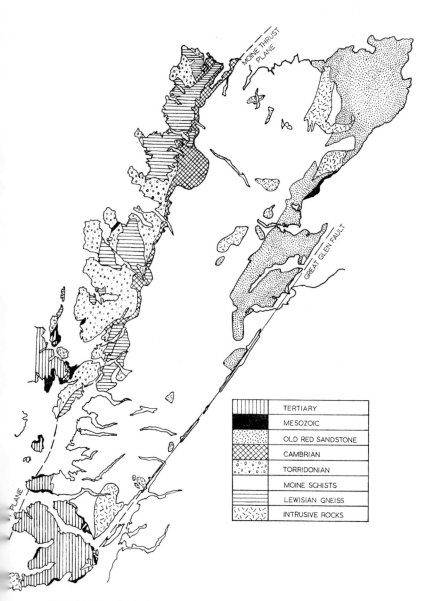

	TERTIARY
	MESOZOIC
	OLD RED SANDSTONE
	CAMBRIAN
	TORRIDONIAN
	MOINE SCHISTS
	LEWISIAN GNEISS
	INTRUSIVE ROCKS

MOINE THRUST PLANE

GREAT GLEN FAULT

PLANE

Simplified geological sketch map of the northern Highlands

were torn off and forced to slide for miles over the adjacent rock. The scars remain today, the greatest being the Moine thrust plane which runs for 120 miles from Skye to the north coast of Sutherland, its course marked by a zone of crushed rock up to 12 miles wide. Assynt is the area to observe this phenomenon and it is possible to see what must have happened deep inside a mountain range while it was being formed. The Great Glen fault and lesser displacements such as the Brora-Helmsdale fault also date from this period although sporadic faulting continued for millions of years afterwards.

In the wake of the earth movements came great upwellings of molten material that solidified to form the igneous rocks of the region, the Strontian granite of Argyll, and the Helmsdale granite and Ben Loyal syenite of Sutherland. From each of these masses veins of finer material pierce the surrounding rocks.

Later Sedimentary Rocks

The Caledonian mountains in their turn were eroded to produce the sediments of the Old Red Sandstone. These now occupy a large part of Caithness and the region of the Cromarty Firth in layer upon layer of yellow, red and grey sandstone and flags, each inch representing many thousands of years of accumulation. The total area and thickness are an indication of how high the Caledonian mountains must have been.

The geography and climate of northern Scotland was vastly different from that of today. From the geological structure, the former existence of a great inland sea can be traced. In 1878 Geikie called it Lake Orcadie. The lake stretched from the present area of the Great Glen to Orkney and Shetland and away out into the North Sea. The water level was not constant; there were periods of drought when the lake shrank to become isolated pools separated by mud flats, the shoreline advancing and retreating, each step preserved in alternating layers of sandstone, shale and mudstone.

The lake teemed with fish whose fossilised remains are tightly

Page 33
Left to right are the peaks of Canisp, Suilven and Cul Mor in west Sutherland, mountains formed of Torridonian sandstone rising from a rough basement of Lewisian gneiss

Page 34
Dunnet Head, most northerly point of the British mainland. Its lighthouse perched above the cliffs of Old Red Sandstone guides ships through the stormy Pentland Firth between Caithness and the Orkney Islands

packed in certain layers of the sediments. Three types of fish are evident: strange jawless creatures like the modern lampreys, a group which may have been the ancestors of our sharks, and a third group that resembled the fish of local waters today. It is an exciting moment to split open a slab of stone and find the clear traces, scales and all, of a fish that swam in Lake Orcadie 350 million years ago. For Hugh Miller, the Cromarty stone-mason, fascination developed into serious scientific study. His book, *The Old Red Sandstone*, published in 1841 created enormous interest and is still regarded as a classic.

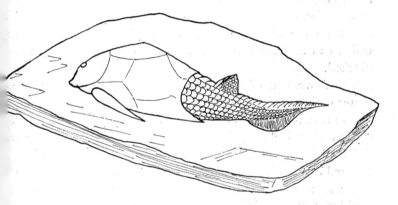

Fossil fish, *Pterichthys milleri*, found in the Old Red Sandstone beds of Caithness and the Cromarty Firth area

Of the still later Mesozoic sediments that occur in patches in Wester Ross and in a long coastal strip between Golspie and Helmsdale, the most important band is the seam of Jurassic coal at Brora. This denotes a period of luxuriant growth and a tropical climate over this part of Scotland. Sediments of Tertiary Age occur in several small outcrops in the western Highlands; but the most characteristic of Tertiary rocks are the volcanic rocks of Skye, Mull and Ardnamurchan.

c

THE LAND

The Ice Age and After

During the last million years the northern hemisphere has suffered long periods of intense cold; ice fields gathered on high ground and spread outwards as glaciers. How often they spread and retreated over Scotland is not certain since later stages in glaciation tend to obliterate the evidence from previous periods. In the Highlands there were at least two major phases in a long period of glaciation.

In the earlier of these phases ice moved outwards from an ice-sheet along the axis of the northern Highlands, its movement largely uninfluenced by topography. Our knowledge of its direction comes from ice scratches on the underlying rocks and from the scattering of boulders of different rock types which can be traced back to the areas from which they were plucked.

The movement of ice across Caithness did not follow this pattern, there being clear evidence of movement from southeast to north-west. This difference is accounted for in the contention that ice moving eastwards off the Highlands was deflected by the Scandinavian ice barrier whose front almost touched Buchan Ness and Caithness. The evidence is difficult to refute since most of Caithness is covered with a bluish-grey boulder clay containing fragments of gneiss from Ross and Cromarty and of Jurassic sandstone not found in Caithness. More interesting, it contains sea-shells that were presumably scooped from the bottom of the Moray Firth. A remarkable example of the carrying power of the ice is the huge block of Cretaceous sandstone found at Leavad, south of Spittal. It measures 240yd by 150yd and is up to 26ft thick. In its passage from the sea-bed off Lybster or Dunbeath it had to cross hills 500ft high.

After the main period of glaciation temperatures began to rise and the ice-cap divided into local glaciers that followed the topography of the region. Each mountain or group of mountains had its own local ice-cap with glaciers flowing down from it into the valleys below, sometimes crossing the paths that earlier glaciers had traced.

About 12,000 years ago the glaciers began to retreat and birch trees colonised the tundra; then in the Boreal period, 4,000 years later, the scrub developed into proper birch and pine forest with a thick undergrowth of hazel. There followed a period of moist, cold climate that destroyed the forests and caused a growth of sphagnum moss but glaciers may well have formed again in the higher glens.

In the warm, wet Atlantic period that is known to have existed from 6000 to 4000 BC, a new birch and pine forest spread northwards while a rapid accumulation of peat occurred in some places. Then came a cooler and drier period when hardwood trees such as the oak and the elm appeared and even the exposed Hebrides had a cover of birch, rowan and hazel. Man was in evidence by this time but there are few early relics in the north-west; he probably found the region unsafe with danger from wolves, bears, moose, lynx, and other creatures. Just before the Christian era, cool wet conditions ensued that were ideal for the development of peat and this rapidly encroached on the forests.

Besides the major climatic changes of the last thousand years there have been lesser fluctuations. When the Vikings made their journeys to Greenland and North America the climate was much less severe than it is now; on the other hand there was a period from the sixteenth century to the mid-eighteenth century which is often referred to as the Little Ice Age on account of its cold winters.

Sea-level fluctuated many times during and after the Ice Age. Traces of a former beach can be found 100ft above present sea-level on the north shore of the Beauly Firth and at Brora and Helmsdale; 50ft and 25ft beaches are extensive around the Dornoch Firth; indeed the whole area between Inverness and Golspie is one of the most remarkable in Scotland for the extent

37

of its raised beaches. Slowly and imperceptibly, changes in sea-level and in climate continue for in Nature nothing is static.

The northern Highlands are relatively poor in minerals yet a surprising variety of materials has been exploited in the past. The traditional building material was stone, quarried from the hillside, and each locality has its own predominant type appearing in houses, farm buildings and dry stone walls. Building stones include the brown and yellow sandstones of the Black Isle, the reddish Torridonian sandstone of Ullapool and the delicate pinky white quartzite that adds such a distinctive touch to the region around Durness and Loch Eriboll. The countryside of Caithness is dominated by flagstones which are easily split into slabs of any desired thickness. They appear as blocks in walls, are used as roofing slates and are set on end in rows as fences.

The Caithness flags are traversed by fractures in which a great variety of minerals have accumulated; some like copper pyrites, galena and zincblende have been worked in the past. There is coal at Brora and alluvial gold near Kildonan; bog iron ore was once worked at Letterewe and mica on the shores of Loch Nevis. The region around Strontian has veins of galena, zincblende, barytes, quartz, celestite and zeolite but the most interesting mineral, discovered here in 1760, was then unknown to science. It was found to contain a new element, Strontium. The mineral itself was given the name strontianite, thus assuring a double connection between science and this small Highland village.

Much of the Highlands is covered with peat, a deposit of partly decomposed plants that develops in cold, water-logged conditions. The crofters of a previous generation derived their fuel from peat bogs. Using a special spade, peat was dug out in blocks, laid flat on the moor for the first stage of drying then set on end in pyramids to dry completely. In late summer the dried peat was brought home either by horse and cart or in baskets on the crofters' backs to be built into a stack behind the croft house. The scent of peat smoke rising white from the chimneys and pervading every corner of the old houses used to be an essential part of the Highland picture. Even today many crofters still burn peat.

Peat is both a challenge and a disappointment to Highland economists. In 1949 the Scottish Peat Committee was set up following the pioneer research of the late Mr G. K. Fraser. They surveyed peat bogs and researched the different ways of utilising this abundant material. £500,000 was spent in building an experimental power station using peat as fuel at Altnabreac in Caithness where a deposit of 13·2 million tons of peat solids had been revealed. The plant closed down in 1960, the actual harvesting of the peat being the greatest problem. The inescapable fact is that peat, with 90 per cent water content, may require more heat to dry it than it will give out when burned.

It is wrong to assess the importance of Highland rocks in economic terms alone. The region has a great attraction for a special kind of visitor, the collector of mineral specimens or the 'rockhound'. Many of the rocks contain accessory minerals which can be classed as semi-precious gemstones, while a few can be classed as precious. Amethyst in six-sided transparent purple crystals is reputed to occur in the Loch Morar area; yellow or pale green beryl occurs at Struy, south of Beauly, where one can also find zircon and almandine garnet; Ross and Cromarty's list includes agate, garnet, jasper, tourmaline, zircon and topaz.

No one really knows the extent of the wealth that still lies buried in the mountains. In 1959 the Geological Survey discovered that the Cambrian beds of shale and dolomite are rich enough in potash to have economic potential. Outcrops extend intermittently from Loch Eriboll to Loch Kishorn and appear again in the south of Skye—a distance of 110 miles. Tests showed an average potash content of 8 per cent with individual tests showing as much as 10 per cent. If a market is found, shipment will be no problem since there is deep water nearby at Loch Eriboll. There are large amounts of crystalline quartz-ite in the basal Cambrian rocks underlying the Durness lime-stone and the dolomite. Most of the samples tested showed impurities at less than 1 per cent. Although remote from present markets, heavy industrial development in Easter Ross may alter the situation.

SCENERY

The northern Highlands are crossed by several sets of fractures and these determine the directions of the hills and valleys of the region. The Caledonian trend runs from north-north-east to south-south-west, a grain that reveals itself especially in the Great Glen and its freshwater lochs and Loch Linnhe. There are other older series of fractures that influence local topo-graphy: in the Lewisian gneiss of the western sea-board a grain runs from north-west to south-east and shows itself in the direction of Loch Assynt and Loch Maree and of the many lochs and streams in between.

The nature of the rocks themselves has an influence on scenery. The Lewisian gneiss stands out among other rocks with its bare domes and ridges, these giving an uneven appearance to the landscape. The Moine schists also give rise to smooth hills, the absence of prominent peaks suggesting an ancient landscape pared to its very foundations. In the mountains around Glen Shiel, however, erosion has proceeded even further and the Moine schists form the highest ground in the region. The Torridonian sandstone is well bedded and jointed and it weathers into rectangular blocks and vertical crags as at Suil-ven, Slioch and An Teallach. One of the most outstanding examples of the relationship between geology and scenery is seen in the hard white capping of quartzite above the plinths of reddish sandstone in Canisp and Quinag. A similar resistant quartzite forms the upland masses of the Scarabens in Caithness.

The major aspects of Highland scenery, however, were produced by the processes of weathering, the gouging of former glaciers, the shattering of present day frost and ice, the action of rain, streams and rivers, and the pounding of the sea. These processes have operated extremely slowly and imperceptibly but extremely efficiently.

Prolonged glaciation has produced deep corries near the mountain tops, smoothed lower slopes and U-shaped valleys, and rock surfaces planed yet heavily scratched by moving ice. The remains of glacial lakes can be seen at Achnasheen while the long ridges near Dornoch, now covered with heather and gorse, were deposited by melting glaciers. The impression is that these are recent features; moraines and drumlins, and large boulders known as erratics, lie just as they were dumped by the melting ice; and in places it is possible to trace the steps of the retreating glacier up the valley by way of its terminal moraines.

Ice is still active in winter, breaking blocks of stone and causing rock splinters to fall as screes around the foot of a precipice. Then in spring the grip of the ice is relaxed and watercourses come to life with mountain streams, the rush of moorland burns and the roar of waterfalls. This is a region of high rainfall where streams flow straight down steep mountain sides and then sweep into beds on the lower slopes where they scatter pebbles and boulders before joining the river in the valley below. The spine of the Highlands runs very near the west coast so that westward-flowing rivers are shorter, more rapid and of greater scouring effect than those flowing towards the North Sea. There are spectacular waterfalls like those of the Corrieshalloch Gorge near Ullapool and the Falls of Glomach near Kylesku. The latter, with a drop of 658ft, is the highest waterfall in Britain. The River Shin is the most impressive of the eastward-flowing rivers, plunging down wild gorges and having its own spectacle in the Falls of Shin.

Even more spectacular than the work of rivers is the work of the sea, battering exposed headlands and undermining the cliffs to create a wealth of coastal features ranging from sheer rocks to gently sloping sandy beaches. The east coast is more regular than that of the west with low cliffs and wide stretches of sandy beaches, the west coast being deeply indented. It is a coastline full of delight with deep narrow fjords and wide open bays dotted with numerous islets, where the waves of the Minch explode in white spray on dark headlands. Some of the most spectacular coastal scenery is found in the sandstone cliffs of Caithness. A cave may be tunnelled along a joint plane and then part of the roof collapse at the inner end to form a blow-hole or gloup like that at Holborn Head. Where two caves meet a natural arch forms like that of the Brig o' Trams; later the whole roof falls to result in a steep-sided stack. The many stacks and skerries lying offshore indicate the slow, relentless advance of the sea.

There are numerous sandy beaches, some of the best occurring on the north shores of the Dornoch Firth. In Caithness the wide sandy sweep of Sinclair's Bay has a great attraction for visitors. Along the north coast the beaches of Dunnet Bay, Melvich Bay, Bettyhill and Balnakiel are among the best, while down the west coast lie Sandwood Bay, Gruinard Bay, Rhu Stoer and Gairloch. Everywhere, beach deposits reflect local geographical differences: at Durness the pinkish white sands are derived from Cambrian quartzite, at Loch Broom the sand is almost chocolate-coloured and the pure white sands of Morar are world famous. At low spring tides rare coral sands are exposed at Tanera Beag in the Summer Isles and at Erbusaig near Kyle of Lochalsh.

The entire Highland region is of great scenic beauty but even here there are areas of exceptional splendour. The region of Inverpolly and Glencanisp Forest in west Sutherland is an area of mountain and loch surmounted by the peaks of Stac Polly, Canisp and Suilven. Suilven rises 2,309ft from a platform of gneiss and has been called the most fantastic mountain in Scotland. The name means 'the Pillar', which is indeed its shape as seen from the west or the east, but from the north and south Suilven appears elongated with steep sides and a rounded top. The peaks of Sutherland are seen to good effect from the deck of a ship in the North Minch—a crowd of mountains in which everyone of them stands out.

The very name of Wester Ross conjures up visions of remote grandeur, of mountains and glens carved in ancient rocks, of short rapid rivers and of placid lochs with pine-clad islets. Each loch has its own character, from the wild beauty of Loch Clair to the serenity of Loch Maree. Some of the wildest scenery in Scotland is found between Little Loch Broom and Loch Maree, especially around the mass of An Teallach with its corries, ridges and numerous peaks and around the lonely Loch Toll an Lochan below the precipitous cliffs of Sail Liath.

Less well known areas also have their devotees. The peninsula of Ardnamurchan is off the main tourist trail yet at Sanna Bay on its north tip is one of Scotland's finest beaches, of shell sand. There are those who find beauty in the windswept plains of Caithness, while for the motorist one of the most spectacular views is from the top of the Ord of Caithness. Another fine view is the first glimpse of Sutherland from Struie Hill, the silver ribbon of the Kyle of Sutherland winding its way between well-wooded hills and the distant peaks of Ben More Assynt dominating the sky-line beyond.

From Lochinver to Kylesku runs one of the most delightful roads in the Highlands. It twists and turns sweeping into steep gradients of 1 in 5 and even 1 in 4 with glimpses of the sea and sandy beaches, of croft houses perched on hilltops, of lochs full of reeds and water-lilies, and of rivers tumbling through ravines, their sides clothed with birch and rowan and overhanging ledges thick with bell heather. But the landscape is dominated by the bare grey and reddish Lewisian gneiss where

43

the ice sheet pared one section of ground to leave a thin cover of soil on another.

The National Trust for Scotland has done a remarkable job since its foundation in 1931 in preserving places of historic interest and of natural beauty. At Torridon the Trust owns over 14,000 acres of some of Scotland's finest mountain scenery and including the seven peaks of Liathach (3,488ft) and Beinn Alligin (3,232ft). Other Trust properties include Corrieshalloch Gorge where the river tumbles 150ft into a gorge one mile long and 200ft deep at the Falls of Measach; the region of Kintail at the head of Loch Duich with the five peaks known as the Sisters of Kintail; and the Balmacara estate which covers most of the Kyle-Plockton peninsula.

Nature reserves also contain and protect much marvellous scenery. Inverpolly Nature Reserve is a glaciated plateau of gneiss and Torridonian sandstone with lochans, bogs, moorland and screes; Beinn Eighe consists of reddish sandstone topped with dazzling white quartzite. Other bodies concerned with preservation are the Countryside Commission for Scotland set up in 1967, and the Nature Conservancy set up in 1949. Although there are no national parks in Scotland some areas of great scenic beauty are subject to strict planning control, close supervision of these areas being maintained by the Secretary of State for Scotland. Two such areas are those around Glen Affric, Glen Cannich and Strathfarrar and around Loch Torridon, Loch Maree and Loch Broom.

Wherever one travels in the Highlands one is struck by the emptiness of mountains and moorland, there are plenty of sheep but few people. Here and there roofless crofts and mounds of stones bear witness to the families who once struggled unsuccessfully to make a living but where the Gaelic place names are the only survivors of a bygone age.

SOILS AND LAND USE

Good soils are scarce in the northern Highlands, most of the area being underlain by hard, acid rocks that do not readily break down. The resulting soil is poor in lime and phosphates and even the low ground is rough with little patches of soil among bare outcrops of schist and gneiss. High rainfall gives rise to large areas of wet moorland and peat bogs. In this type of country sheep farming is the most common form of land use, each crofter having the right to pasture a certain number of sheep on the common grazings. On the gneiss of Sutherland and Ross and Cromarty there is much poor grass and sedge, but there are acres of bare quartzite with hardly any plants at all. Here, even sheep farming is difficult and there are large tracts suitable only for red deer. Deer forest and common grazing often overlap and some areas like the peaks of Arkle and Suilven can graze sheep in summer but not in winter. In the drier eastern moorlands grouse are important for their sporting value and feed on the extensive cover of heather.

In the extreme north-west there are several fertile strips of land along the patches of limestone at Elphin, Knockan, Sangomore and Eriboll, green valleys contrasting with the bleak hills on either side. Along the north coast there are several localities where sand blowing inland from the beaches has lightened the soil to create green sward and fertile fields but nothing matches the long stretch of machair of the Hebrides. In the extreme south the basalt lavas of Morvern are good soil producers but they need careful handling as they can dry out if overworked.

Glacial drift is an important soil producer although it is poor in comparison with similar deposits in other parts of Scotland. It absorbs heavy rainfall, can produce good pasture and is suitable for forestry. The western slopes of the Highlands are steep and little glacial debris was retained there but large amounts accumulated on the more gentle eastern slopes. There were old glacial lakes at Achnasheen and in the valley of the River Oykell where sheep now find good grazing over level stretches of drift.

The best soils of all occur in Caithness and on the coastal strip north of Inverness. Here the parent rock is Old Red Sandstone which breaks down into good soil. The visitor to Ross-shire cannot fail to be impressed by the difference between the well-tilled fields of the Black Isle and the rugged mountains of Wester Ross. Another example of the control of geology over soils and vegetation is seen on the north coast where the green fields of the Caithness plain give way to heather- and bracken-covered hills.

The nature of the parent rock is only one factor in the production of soil: climate is just as important. The dominant factor in the Highlands is the high rainfall sluicing down steep hillsides, washing away soil particles and baring the underlying rock, a process that is most marked along the west coast. The mildness of the west is another factor against good soil since winter precipitation in the east is held as snow into late spring.

While soil, climate and relief dictate the nature of the primary vegetation it is man who, within these limits, controls the secondary vegetation. His effect is considerable. Forests have been cut down to produce arable land, the natural layers of the soil are mixed by the plough, and lands once under natural grass or forest now support commercial forests or fields of oats, barley and grass of species of the farmer's own choosing.

Even peat bogs which once supported only coarse heather and white tufts of cotton grass can have their pasture improved to increase the production of sheep. Pasture improvement takes two forms. Where there is already a nucleus of good grass or clover, drainage and the addition of lime and fertilizers can work wonders but where vegetation cannot be improved reseeding is necessary. Where deep ploughing is not feasible surface seeding with lime and manure can achieve much but the best results occur where the existing vegetation is killed by deep ploughing, pioneer crops of rape or turnips are grazed by sheep to build up fertility, and then after further cultivation the final grass mixture is sown.

Just as the land may be improved, so may it be allowed to deteriorate. The old croft lands, once cleared so laboriously by hand and then delved or ploughed each year, are now untilled but grazed heavily by sheep. Sheep, unlike cattle, are selective feeders, eating out the finest grass and leaving the coarser types to seed and spread. There is no doubt that the present high sheep to cattle ratio is causing deterioration of the pasture.

In these days when there is such pressure on land elsewhere in Britain it is imperative that better use is made of the Highlands. At one time farming was regarded as the most important form of land use: the forests shrank and the range of wild animals diminished to provide more fields and better grazing for livestock. Attitudes have changed and land use is now an important science, the emphasis being on multiple land use with farming, forestry, tourism, sport and wildlife conservation all integrated into a comprehensive pattern. Sometimes it is difficult to maintain a balance between competing elements whether it be farming and forestry or farming and wildlife conservation. No one can deny that the red deer occupies a prominent place in the Highlands—it attracts visitors, its sporting value is considerable and there is a growing export trade in venison. But the population of red deer must be controlled if farmers are not to suffer predatory animals in excess. So far it has not been found necessary to control tourists but it is becoming clear that the large numbers of people now visiting the Highlands will soon constitute a problem. Already, campers and caravanners have caused damage to the binding vegetation on sand dunes at Morar and Durness.

In the eastern lowlands the problems are of a different nature. Here the competing elements are the demands of housing and heavy industry on good farm land. It is obvious that each is important and must be encouraged; the problem is how to integrate them. Under the Town and Country Planning Act of

47

1947 local authorities were given extensive powers in the siting of industry, the protection of agriculture and forestry and the conservation of the countryside but the quickening pace of oil-related activities may undermine even the wisest moves of the past. Nowhere is wise planning for the future more important than on the shores of the Cromarty Firth. It is essential to learn from the mistakes of the first Industrial Revolution and avoid their repetition in the Industrial Revolution of the Highlands.

2   *FLORA AND FAUNA*

MANY rare species of plants and animals flourish in the vastness and remoteness of the northern Highlands. This is rapidly becoming the most favoured area in Britain for natural historians and is a region of unfathomed mysteries, the monsters of Loch Ness and Loch Morar still attracting serious investigators. No one has yet disproved the possibility that some creature believed to be long extinct survives in the dark unexplored depths of these lochs.

FLORA

Much of the northern Highlands is rough and poorly drained, its vegetation consisting mainly of coarse grass, sedge and rushes that barely clothe the underlying rocks but which in autumn paint the landscape in vivid yellows, greens and gold. Moorland flowers are small but brightly coloured and highly scented. The ground is sprinkled with the yellow stars of bog asphodel, the lilac flowers of spotted orchid, the pale blue of dog violet and marsh violet, while deep purple bell heather (*Erica cinerea*) grows in clumps among the rocks. On peat moorland the dominant vegetation is cross-leaved heather (*Erica tetralix*) with more than a dozen varieties of sphagnum moss but the monotony is broken by the white tufts of cotton grass. On the gneiss country of the north-west shallow lochans are almost choked with water lobelia and water-lilies floating among the reeds.

On the drier, eastern side of the Highlands the heather moors are a blaze of purple in autumn. This is usually the work of a single species (*Calluna vulgaris*) but in places is associated with bell heather, cowberry, lichens and mosses. Although regarded as so typical of Scotland, ecologists maintain that the heather moors are not in their natural state and are the result of forests being cleared by axe and fire especially since the introduction of sheep less than 200 years ago.

On mountain tops, above the peat, a different flora is encountered—plants that can withstand high winds and low temperatures and alternating periods of drought and saturation. Here the hand of man has been withheld and the mountain tops contain survivals from the period following the last Ice Age. From similarities elsewhere in the world this is known as an arctic-alpine assemblage.

The woolly hair moss (*Rhacomitrium lanuginosum*) is the most successful plant here and where it is well established a thin layer of soil forms which in turn encourages other plants like crowberry and bearberry. There are also a few rare flowers: among alpine grasses and sedges are sea-pink, purple saxifrage, starry saxifrage, alpine saxifrage, and alpine forget-me-not, while thyme can be found as high as 3,000ft. On rock ledges where deer and sheep cannot gain access heath violet and sheep's bit scabious bloom. Trees are scarce but the dwarf juniper grows in the lee of large stones and boulders. Alpine flowers occur at progressivly lower altitudes as one goes north and at Cape Wrath they occur almost at sea-level.

The lowland pastures and cultivated areas contain an astonishing variety of wild flowers, one of the most unforgettable sights in spring and early summer being the yellow glare of gorse and broom. As summer advances the fields glow with buttercups and the roadside ditches are gay with gowan, vetch and the harebell (*Campanula rotundifolia*), the Scottish 'bluebell'. The limestone areas have their own special plants such as starry and yellow mountain saxifrage, moss campion and the mountain avens, locally called 'the rose of Assynt'. The rare globe flower can be seen at Elphin and Knockan.

A bird that is still very rare, except in the most remote regions; a golden eagle watches protectively over its young in a mountain eyrie

Page 52
Loch Maree in Ross and Cromarty, one of the most beautiful of Scotland's lochs, with steep-sided Slioch (3,260ft) like a fortress guarding its southern end. In the foreground is a stand of conifers planted by the Forestry Commission

Rivers and lochs have a distinctive flora with reeds and bulrushes, horsetails and marestails growing along their marshy edges, ferns in shady places, and wild rose and foxglove on secluded ledges along their banks. One of the earliest flowers to bloom in spring is the marsh marigold which transforms sluggish water courses into ribbons of gold. The short rivers of Caithness have some interesting plants, especially the holy grass. When crushed this plant gives off the sweet scent of new-mown hay and its name comes from the Scandinavian custom of scattering it on the floor of churches to sweeten the air. Once known in south-west Scotland, it was believed to be extinct until the Caithness botanist, Robert Dick, rediscovered it growing along the banks of the Thurso River.

The sea-shore has a fascinating flora, plants which have adapted to the special conditions of periods of drought and periods of flying spray. Special adaptations are seen in rose root, English stone crop, scurvy grass and marram grass which are all able to absorb moisture when it is available and to store it until it is required. These plants all have a shiny waterproof surface to eliminate evaporation of moisture. A typical plant of the sea-shore is thrift or sea-pink which grows in low clumps so as to lessen damage by wind. Certain plants of the sea-shore such as orache and bladder campion adapt to their salty environment by developing thick, fleshy leaves.

The loose sand of the dunes along the north coast is stabilised by a mat of marram grass. Inland this gives way to a fine turf with a rich and varied flora, the bright yellow of bird's foot tre-foil contrasting with the more subdued white and helio of eye-bright and the purple of wild thyme. On Reay Links there is a type of eyebright which occurs nowhere else in the world—its botanic name is *Euphrasia brevipila reayensis*. Another rare flower of wider range although restricted to the north of Scotland is the mauve primrose (*Primula scotica*), best known as the emblem of the Scottish Wildlife Trust.

Plant life extends even to high-water mark. Mingled with

D

the flotsam of winter storms are the thick leaves of sea sandwort and oyster plant, the lilac flowers of sea rocket and the fragrant yellow flowers of silverweed.

The Forests

The forests account for some of the most beautiful stretches of the northern Highlands but these are only fragments of the extensive forests that existed before man came to pursue his policy of destruction. Attitudes have changed fortunately and thousands of acres of once barren moorland now support thriving stands of conifers planted by the Forestry Commission. But the old forest can never be restored and the portions still surviving are part of a priceless heritage to be preserved at all costs.

In the richer soils and more sheltered valleys of the west, the main species is oak; in the exposed north of the country the more hardy birch predominates; but the largest area, a wedge of country which narrows westwards from the Great Glen, grows pine with a mixture of birch and oak.

The Scots Pine is the typical tree of the Highlands with its bright bottle-green foliage, its short needles and distinctive red boughs. The best surviving fragments of the old pine forest are at Coille na Glas Leitire on the shores of Loch Maree, in Glenstrathfarrar and at the wood of Coulin in Glen Torridon. The pine-covered islands of Loch Maree also show what the old forest was like. Where sunlight penetrates the roof of foliage the floor of a pine forest is covered in ling and bell heather but in the darker areas blaeberry and cowberry are dominant and shade-loving plants such as winter green and wood anemone are common.

The ancient oak woods were concentrated in the south-west, but with fingers extending up the Great Glen and along the coast to Wester Ross. Unfortunately the surviving remnants are very scattered, small patches being found along the shores of Loch Lochy, Loch Arkaig and Loch Ness. There are patches of oak at Ariundle in Sunart and at Ardnamurchan while the most northerly remnant occurs at Letterewe. Former oakwoods near Gairloch were felled for boat-building in the nineteenth century. An oak wood has a rich and varied associated flora being interspersed with hazel, ash and holly. The ground is usually covered with moss and bracken and where the sheep cannot gain access there are sheets of bluebells (*Scilla nutans*).

Birch forests are more hardy and extend up the mountain sides to a level of 2,000ft, degenerating northwards into a birch scrub with subsidiary hazel. There are large stretches of birch with hazel and alder in Inverpolly forest, below the north face of Quinag and at the head of Loch Eriboll. The birch-covered islets of Loch Sionascaig remind the visitor of what the old forest must have looked like. The rowan tree with its clusters of red berries in autumn is a common subsidiary of birch forests. The forest floor is usually covered with moss, spleenwort, wood sorrel, primroses and violets.

Within the broad picture there are variations and again the limestone areas have special associations. On the limestone areas of Durness and at the head of Loch Kishorn there are forests of ash with hazel and hawthorn, while at Allt nan Carnan gorge in Wester Ross there is a mixed woodland of oak, birch and Scots pine with hazel, ash, rowan, wych elm and bird cherry. Under natural conditions species of trees are mixed although one may be dominant. This contrasts with the practice of foresters to grow neat stands of trees of a single species, a practice which is now being re-examined in the light of a poor associated fauna. Around Loch Sunart lie some of the best examples of mixed forest in Scotland.

FAUNA

As in the case of the flora, man has had a pronounced effect on the animal life of the region but it is still rich and varied, ranging from Britain's largest land mammal, the red deer, to the smallest, the pygmy shrew. Here the wild cat still flourishes, the pine marten, fox and badger are common and it is believed that the pole cat may still survive in remote places.

The pine marten was once confined to north-west Sutherland but its numbers have increased greatly since the 1920s and it is now common all over the northern Highlands. The badger is also increasing but was once more numerous as commemorated by placenames such as Càrn a' Brochd in Torridon where it is now locally extinct. The blue or mountain hare is common although its numbers fluctuate violently from time to time. Rabbits are common once again on drier slopes in spite of being almost wiped out by myxomatosis in the late 1950s. The domestic goat readily reverts to a wild state and there are herds of these feral goats living above the peat line. Their young are born in the harsh conditions of January and February.

The forests have their own group of animals in squirrels, mice, voles and shrews. The red squirrel is particularly common now although almost extinct in the eighteenth century. In 1844 Lady Lovat introduced red squirrels to the grounds of Beaufort Castle, Beauly, and this stock fanned out to recolonise Sutherland and spread along the Great Glen, part going westwards to Loch Broom. Now the red squirrel is a forest pest and there are attempts to control it by shooting.

The sea supports two types of seal, the common seal and the grey or Atlantic seal. For a long time both species were important to man for their skins, meat and oil. The grey seal was the more vulnerable since it spends much of its life ashore on remote islands for mating, calving and moulting but since 1914 it has been protected by law. The life of the grey seal is described in detail by Dr Frank Fraser Darling in his book *Natural History in the Highlands and Islands*. Some species of whales, too, came near to extinction in the first decades of this century. The blue whale and sperm whale, no longer molested, are found west of the Hebrides while the common rorqual, lesser rorqual and porpoise are common off the north and west coasts. Equally at home on land or sea is the otter and this region was made famous by Gavin Maxwell who described his life with otters in his book *Ring of Bright Water*.

There are several types of deer in this area. The fallow deer was introduced about a thousand years ago and is found in several localities including Rosehall in Sutherland and Berriedale in Caithness. The sika deer, a native of Japan, was introduced to the Highlands at Achanalt Forest in Ross-shire in 1889, since when it has spread considerably. The lovely roe deer, a shy creature of the forests, has been a native of the northern Highlands since prehistoric times.

The animal that most typifies the Highlands is the red deer. There are $2\frac{1}{2}$ million acres of deer forest in the Highlands, most of it north and west of the Great Glen. Controversy surrounds the large amount of land reserved for deer but it must be pointed out that at least 90 per cent of this figure is poor ground over 2,000ft with much bare rock covered with snow in winter and supporting poor grass and sedge in summer. On this type of ground there is no animal more successful than the red deer.

For our knowledge of the life of the red deer we are most indebted to Dr Frank Fraser Darling whose pioneering work carried out in Ross-shire between 1933 and 1936 is recorded in his classic *A Herd of Red Deer*. He describes the pains he took to become acquainted with these lovely creatures, how he walked barefoot during the summer of 1935 and discovered that after a fortnight of discomfort 'the whole threshold of awareness was raised'. In his book Dr Fraser Darling describes their movements over the year, the influence of weather from summer heat to winter snow, and the daily rhythm with periods of rest and feeding.

Dr Fraser Darling believes that the red deer have reached the highest development of sociality of all grazing animals. Their social system is a matriarchy founded on the family, for however majestic the stag in the mating season he never attains the status of leader, this being the prerogative of an old hind.

For over 10 months of the year the mature stags form their

own groups and during the summer they graze by themselves high up in the mountains to avoid midges and clegs. In April and May the old antlers drop off but the new ones start to grow immediately, first as bumps and then branching repeatedly until the full 'head' is seen still covered with a thick skin known as velvet. It is difficult to understand what use these antlers are to the stag. However attractive as an ornament in a stately home they are an encumbrance to the animal, their annual growth in a lime-deficient country being a serious drain on the red deer, causing it to devour cast-off antlers and eat the velvet peeling from its own and other deers' antlers. They do have an important significance during the rut, in sexual stimulation and in fighting.

In August the stags prepare for their short mating season. Many changes occur in the animals themselves: their necks thicken, their manes grow longer and fights break out over ownership of hinds. The artist Landseer was particularly impressed by this and his painting 'Monarch of the Glen' shows a stag at bay, his mouth open in the characteristic roar of challenge, anger and lust.

In early November the rut ends and the stags resume their separate existence. Both sexes winter on low ground and when snow threatens long lines of them make their way to the valley floor. Calves are born from late May to July with a peak in the first three weeks of June, the calves lying alone for two to five days until strong enough to follow their mother. It is at this stage that they are most vulnerable to enemies such as the wild cat, golden eagle and fox, but particularly the latter. If the hind is short of milk in the autumn there is little hope of the calf surviving the winter. Losses of calves and old animals are also heavy in spring.

The importance of the red deer is now fully recognised. The Deer (Scotland) Act of 1959 established closed seasons during which deer cannot be hunted. The Red Deer Commission was set up and it immediately organised a country-wide census to determine the optimum culling rate, fixed at a rate of one-sixth each year. Assuming an adult red deer population of 150,000 in Scotland, the maximum crop is thus about 25,000 carcases a year. These earned almost £500,000 in 1972. The true value of these creatures cannot be assessed in terms of money alone and research into the red deer has also been carried out by the universities of Edinburgh and Aberdeen and by the Rowett Research Institute. The British Deer Society, inaugurated in 1963, seeks to stimulate interest among the public.

Birds

There are many unexpected visitors to delight bird watchers on the lonely Highland moors. Golden plovers in particular frequent the moors with lapwings on the grasslands. The cuckoo is common in summer using the meadow pipit as foster parent. On the drier heather moors the red grouse is the most important bird and many thousands of acres are managed for sport. It is a hardy bird and may sit buried under snow on its clutch of 15 eggs. Its main diet is young shoots of heather. The black grouse, less common and disappearing in many places, is a bird of scrub rather than of open moor. In spring the males gather at traditional places known as leks where they join in a ceremonial 'dance' before mating with the hens.

Moorland lochs have their own species of birds and one of the most beautiful is the Slavonian grebe, its glossy black head slashed with a broad golden stripe which ends in a tuft behind the neck. As beautiful is the red-throated diver which nests close to the edge of the water. The lochs are frequented by the dipper and the goosander while boggy islands often support a colony of black-headed gulls or a pair of teal or widgeon.

On the marshes around the lochs the greenshank is found and once heard, his strange haunting call is never forgotten. This is really a bird of sub-arctic forests yet it nests on the treeless moors of north-west Scotland, sharing its habitat with red-shank, green sandpiper and common sandpiper.

59

The high mountain tops have some rare residents. The ptarmigan breeds on barren slopes and the snow bunting among boulders at around 3,oooft. Numbers of ptarmigan are kept low by the golden eagle which hunts here from his eyrie on crags lower down the mountains. The golden eagle is reputed to kill lambs since their carcases are to be found in eagles' nests, but closer examination reveals the identity of the killer—the ears chewed off by a fox, the eyes picked out by a crow. There is no doubt that Scotland's golden eagles are one of the rarities of Europe.

For their variety of birds, the forests are hard to beat. The pine forests shelter flocks of Scottish crossbills and Scottish crested tits—both relics of the post-glacial pine forests and different in some ways from their European counterparts. Another forest bird is the capercaillie, living on the shoots of spruce and larch and the buds of Scots pine. This bird was extinct about 1770 but re-introduced in the mid-nineteenth century. The list of forest dwellers is impressive and includes the siskin, goldcrest, blue tit, crested tit, tree creeper, robin, tree pipit, chaffinch, wood pigeon, bullfinch, willow warbler and wood warbler. A common bird of prey in the forests is the tawny owl but sparrow hawks and merlins are now rare. The great spotted woodpecker became extinct as a breeding species about 1850 but returned at the turn of the century and now breeds in most parts of the Highlands.

For sheer numbers of birds, however, the sea-shore is most impressive, especially the cliffs and stacks of Caithness where guillemots, razorbills, kittiwakes and puffins nest in the horizontal ledges of Old Red Sandstone. As impressive are the great sea-bird cities of Handa Island and the high cliffs of Clo Mor. In June 1969 a bird count on the cliffs at Clo Mor revealed 3,000 pairs of fulmars, 1,200 pairs of kittiwakes and over 20,000 pairs of guillemots. From the top of the cliffs streams of gannets can be seen passing far below, while at times a golden eagle drifts overhead. The best time to visit the sea-bird colonies is in

June when every ledge is occupied, eggs are hatching out, parent birds are constantly on the wing and the puffin returns from a fishing trip with four or five small fish hanging from his brightly coloured bill. Handa Island is now run as a bird sanctuary by the RSPB. A hundred years ago man gave up the struggle to live here but birds continue to thrive in the terraces of Torridonian sandstone.

The estuaries of the Dornoch Firth, the Cromarty Firth, and the Beauly Firth are winter feeding grounds for many species of duck. The total number of widgeon in the Cromarty Firth is about 25,000 and in the Beauly Firth about 10,000. Other ducks present are mallard, teal and pintail, shelduck, red-breasted merganser, goosander, common scoter, long-tailed duck and goldeneye. It is vitally important that these feathered inhabitants are taken into consideration when plans are drawn up for industrial development.

Birds are highly independent in answering the call of migration, some to winter in warmer lands and others in the Highlands. Some fly north to nest in the Arctic. But nothing is static and no habit entirely predictable. Within the last two decades of a cooling northern climate at least a dozen species have found conditions suitable to start nesting and these include the great northern diver, goldeneye, fieldfare and brambling. Even more outstanding is the spread of the fulmar petrel. In 1878 its only British breeding station was St Kilda, from where it spread to Shetland, then south to Orkney and along the north coast into the Minch. By 1929 it was nesting on the island of Tiree. Once exclusively a cliff dweller it can now be found nesting in old quarries and even on the roofs of Highland castles. Probably better known is the case of the collared dove which made a rapid spread northwards over Britain and by 1965 had begun nesting in Shetland.

Fish of River, Loch and Sea

The brown trout (*Salmo trutta*) is widely distributed in lochs and streams throughout the northern Highlands. It feeds on larvae and adult caddis flies, wind-blown midges and aquatic beetles. There is, however, another form of *Salmo trutta*, the migratory form known as sea trout which is hatched in small streams like the sedentary form but which, when between two and four years old, begins to move downstream towards the sea. In the brackish water of the estuaries it develops a silver skin before taking completely to the sea and may range far afield before coming back to its own river to spawn.

The salmon is a special fish, the right to fish it being owned and carefully guarded by Highland landowners who let out the right to set nets along the shore. The salmon spawns on gravel beds in the upper stretches of the rivers and the young, known as parr, remain in fresh water for two or three years before migrating to the sea. Some return after only one year as grilse to spawn but others stay away for up to four years before returning as adult salmon. The salmon is the fish typically associated with the Highlands and attracts anglers and sightseers every autumn. The Thurso River is famous for its runs of grilse and one of the great Highland spectacles is the sight of salmon leaping up the Falls of Shin.

Other species of fish frequent Highland lochs—the char in Loch Stack, Loch More and Loch Loyne, pike up to 40lb in weight in Loch Cluanie and Loch Garve, while Loch Ness is noted for its eels. The fresh water pearl mussel was once common in rivers such as the Kerry and Polly in Wester Ross and the Laxford in Sutherland, but they have been overfished.

Coastal waters abound with pelagic and demersal species of fish. Pelagic species include herring, sprat and mackerel while demersal species include haddock, whiting, cod, hake, saithe, skate, plaice, dab and even the elusive halibut. Shellfish include crab, lobster, escallops and prawns, all of which are fished. The basking shark is still common in the Minch in summer. A shark fishery was carried out by Gavin Maxwell from the island of Soay between 1946 and 1949, and his harpooner Tex Geddes carried on in the season 1950–1 but could not compete with the faster, better equipped Norwegian shark boats. Maxwell and Geddes learnt much about the habits of these great fish and each wrote a book on his experiences.

The foreshore is a fascinating place. Between the high and low water marks one catches a tantalising glimpse of a world normally hidden to man of green, red and purple sea-weed, sponges, sea-anemones, crabs and marine worms. Shellfish are abundant and the winkles, cockles and mussels were once an essential part of the diet of the Highlander.

MAN AND NATURE

Since man arrived in the northern Highlands many species of animals and birds have become extinct. It was perhaps understandable that fierce animals like the brown bear and wild boar should be killed and that the killing of the last wolf near Inverness in 1743 was regarded as an achievement, but why should the crane and bittern, the goshawk and osprey have disappeared? The last great auk was killed at St Kilda in 1840 and the white tailed eagle finally died out in 1911. The list of destruction is appalling but man's greatest effect on the Highlands was undoubtedly the clearing of the great Caledonian forests.

It is claimed that the Vikings began to burn these forests during raids after AD 800, but the Highlanders themselves continued the work in their campaign against wolves, and General Monk hated the forests because they harboured rebels. The period of economic exploitation had already begun and in the seventeenth century the forests of Letterewe were felled to provide charcoal for iron smelting. In the nineteenth century the birch forests near Loch Sunart were felled by the bobbin makers at Salen who supplied the cotton mills of Lancashire. Then came the sheep farmers who burned and ring barked the trees to provide more pasture for their flocks.

Even unintentionally man can have an adverse effect on

nature. Intensive grazing by sheep is preventing the regenera-
tion of birch, willow, hazel and gorse; fire can be beneficial in
destroying the old, hard, woody stems of heather, and 'muirburn' is an accepted practice in the Highlands, but too often
the burning is too severe, damaging the surface of the peat,
baring rock outcrops and starting erosion. The spread of
bracken is encouraged all the time. Heather burning stimulates
the growth of young shoots as food for grouse and in the drier
eastern Highlands it has the desired effect. In the west it has
proved disastrous and kills off the heather in favour of the
competitive deer hair grass, and cotton grass, resulting in an
actual decrease in numbers of grouse.

Nineteenth-century landowners regarded wild life as consisting of two classes—those of value to them for sport or food such
as deer and grouse, were encouraged, all the others were classed
as vermin, and discouraged. Premiums were paid at the rate of
10 shillings for the head and talons of an eagle while the face and
ears of a wild cat, pine marten or polecat fetched one shilling.
Osgood Mackenzie in his book *A Hundred Years in the Highlands*
describes the butchery of wildlife—'There was so much vermin
in those days that the so-called game keepers were in reality
only game killers . . . The vermin consisted of all kinds of beasts
and birds, a good many of which are extinct.'

Even today farming methods are hard on wildlife; the call of
the corncrake is now seldom heard, and the use of insecticides,
and chemicals in sheep dips is blamed for the decline in the
numbers of hawks and eagles. Since the use of dieldrin in sheep
dips was banned in 1966 twice as many west Highland eagles
have successfully reared their young. Wanton damage continues with muirburn extending to ledges which are a sanctuary
for rare birds and plants. In the lowlands too, in the name of
farming efficiency, little patches of scrub that harboured a rich
flora and fauna are now being brought under the plough. But
man's record is not all bad for the spread of the pine marten,
crossbill, great spotted woodpecker, roe deer and red squirrel

can all be attributed to tree planting by the Forestry Commission.

Wildlife Conservation

Man has long tried to control nature for his own interests with his management of deer forests and grouse moors, but there is now a real interest in wildlife for its own sake and an anxiety to preserve what is left. The formation of the Nature Conservancy in 1949 and the setting aside of areas as nature reserves were huge steps forward. The land is either purchased by the Nature Conservancy or managed by agreement with the owners. Sites of scientific interest are also designated by the Nature Conservancy but local authorities have the power to adopt their own local nature reserves.

Under the Protection of Birds Act of 1954 and its later amendments, all wild birds, except for a few classified as farmers' pests that may be killed by authorised persons, are protected during their nesting season. Rare birds listed under section one of the act are protected by special penalties against disturbance which even includes the setting up of a photographic hide. Birds on the list include corncrake, red-throated diver and merlin.

Independent bodies play as important a part in the protection of wildlife as does state control. The National Trust for Scotland has purchased Torridon estate, an area rich in wildlife; the Scottish Wildlife Trust, set up in 1964, establishes wild-life refuges supplementary to the reserves of the Nature Conservancy; and the Royal Society for the Protection of Birds administers bird reserves such as Handa Island.

It is not sufficient merely to set apart areas for the conservation of wildlife, since the balance now maintained between certain species is an artificial one created by man. Control must remain in the hands of man but the real problem is how to integrate competing land use and to control nature both for the good of man and the continuance of other species.

3   **EARLY HISTORY**

THE story of man in the northern Highlands goes back to the end of the Ice Age when animals followed the retreating glaciers northwards to be followed in turn by parties of Palaeolithic hunters. A limestone cave at Inchnadamph, discovered in 1926, provides evidence of just such a hunting party with the bones of the animals they killed—reindeer, cave bear and lynx. Animals of arctic regions were then living in Scotland. From the later Mesolithic or Middle Stone Age period much more evidence is available, the people being nomads who fished and hunted but knew nothing of farming. Mesolithic sites have been identified at Keiss and Freswick in Caithness.

THE FIRST SETTLERS

One of the great economic revolutions the world has ever seen occurred when man discovered the art of farming and animal husbandry. This way of life began in the Near East and spread gradually across Europe to reach the Highlands about 5,000 years ago. Unfortunately nothing remains of the houses and our picture of life in Neolithic times is a composite one drawn from the Scottish mainland and the northern isles. These farmers grew barley as a staple crop and kept cattle and sheep. Their single-roomed dwellings were circular or oval in shape and built either of wood or stone depending on the availability of timber. In the centre of the hut was the fireplace, the smoke escaping through a hole in the roof. The simple furniture consisted of stone shelves, cupboards and beds, the latter probably filled with heather or straw or lined with sheep skins. Articles found at Neolithic sites include pottery, stone axes, leaf-shaped flint arrowheads, flint knives, ceremonial stone mace heads and ornamental beads of jet and stone.

Best known of Neolithic structures are the tombs, for however simple the way of life, elaborate procedures were followed for burial of the dead. The tombs were stone-walled with a passage leading to a chamber where successive burials took place. The whole structure was covered with a huge mound of earth or stones and hence the name by which these tombs are known—chambered cairns. Around a hundred of them are known in the north of Scotland, with a concentration along the eastern coastal strip and especially in Caithness.

The Caithness chambered tombs can be divided into two main types, the long cairn and the round cairn. The long cairns are wedge shaped in plan and vary in length from 55 to 240ft. At one end they have semi-circular fore-courts with corners prolonged into 'horns'. The round cairn is by far the most common type in Caithness and varies in diameter from 28 to 75ft. The chambers of both long and round cairns are divided by slabs of stone into three or more compartments and examples of both types can be seen at Camster and Shebster.

At the northern end of the Great Glen there is still another

The round cairn of Camster, Caithness

type of tomb, the Clava tomb which is circular in plan with a circular chamber. Some of them have no entrance and so must have been used only once. We can discuss the size and shape of these tombs but can never know their real significance or the strange religious beliefs that made these early settlers take such pains to provide for their dead.

There is no clear break between the Stone Age and the Bronze Age in the Highlands. It is possible that owing to remoteness the Neolithic way of life persisted long after the use of bronze was known in southern Scotland. Sometime in the third millennium BC, however, a new group of settlers arrived here and from a study of their burials it is clear that they were of a different race from their predecessors. The newcomers brought with them implements of imported flint but articles of bronze are found in a few of their burials. Another innovation was burial in urns or 'beakers' and these early Bronze Age people are usually known as the 'Beaker Folk'.

Most important of Bronze Age remains are the standing stones of Caithness. These are found in various arrangements: single monoliths like those at Reay and Watten, pairs of standing stones as at Latheron and Loch of Yarrows, stone rings as at Guidebest and Broubster, but most outstanding are the stone rows, especially the 200 standing stones at Mid Clyth which are arranged in twenty-two parallel lines.

A stone circle 58ft in diameter and dating from around 1600 BC stands at Raigmore near Inverness. In 1973 when the A9 was being re-routed between Inverness and Invergordon, the stones were moved and a marvellous opportunity was afforded for the circle to be examined in detail. Traces of a Stone Age settlement were found dating from about 3000 BC and with flints and pieces of pottery of a type previously known only from Skara Brae in Orkney. There were traces of graves but the skeletons had long since disintegrated.

Professor Alexander Thom has produced some interesting theories to explain why the standing stones were erected. He

The ruins of Sinclair
and Girnigoe castles
in Caithness, which
were once associated
with the Earls of
Caithness. Castle
Sinclair, the more
modern and dating
from the seventeenth
century, is now
entirely ruinous, but
part of castle Girni-
goe, which dates
from about 1500,
still stands

Page 70
The ruins of Urquhart castle overlooking Loch Ness. Between 1160 and 1398 this castle changed hands at least 16 times. It ceased to be a royal fortress in 1509 but was occupied by the troops of William of Orange and his queen, Mary, who blew it up in 1692 to prevent it falling into the hands of the Jacobites

has proved that those who laid them out had a remarkable knowledge of mathematics and astronomy but their real function is likely to remain a fascinating puzzle.

IRON AGE FORT BUILDERS

Two distinct types of Iron Age fortress survive in the Highlands, built by two separate races of people. In the north and west stand the brochs, and ruins of vitrified forts are found along the Great Glen.

The brochs are the best known of all prehistoric structures in the north of Scotland. Built entirely without mortar they represent the highest development of dry stone building in Western Europe. Best preserved of all brochs is that on the Shetland island of Mousa which is complete to the original wall-head. From a study of this and remnants elsewhere, it is clear that a typical broch was bell-shaped, wide at ground level then narrowing upwards and finally rising straight to a height of 40ft or more. At ground level the diameter was about 60ft with walls 15ft or so thick enclosing a central courtyard where a group of families could live in safety. The lower part of the wall was solid but higher up it was hollow, the space being occupied by a succession of low galleries running round the tower, the galleries being reached by a spiral stairway also within the wall. It has been suggested that the brochs were the forts of a conquering race but the plan of a broch suggests a defensive rather than an offensive role. The walls are designed to make scaling impossible and there is only one opening, a low passage that could quickly be barricaded from within.

Brochs are confined almost exclusively to the north of Scotland, to Caithness, Sutherland, Ross and Cromarty and the islands of Skye, Orkney and Shetland. Of the 600 or so recorded sites about a quarter of them occur in Caithness. This distribution suggests a race of people—a well defined political unit, rare at that time—pushed into the northern extremities of Scotland.

E

The broch of Dun Dornadilla, Sutherland

Who was the enemy that caused this spate of fort-building? J. R. C. Hamilton in his book *The Northern Isles* suggests that it was the Celtic invaders from the north of England who built their own forts in a belt across central Scotland and along the Great Glen about 100 BC.

The Iron Age was a time of deteriorating climate and saw the onset of the more stormy sub-Atlantic period. These wet conditions favoured the development of peat which spread over the arable land and the pasture of former agricultural areas. The resulting land hunger in northern Europe stirred up the tribes and caused large-scale migrations. The advance of Roman legions across Europe probably helped to create unsettled conditions.

How long the emergency lasted is not known. The end of broch building can be dated from the discovery of second-century Roman coins in post-broch dwelling-houses. Mr Hamilton suggests that the victory of the Romans over the Caledonians at Mons Graupius in AD 83 removed the threat from the southern enemy. He also makes the intriguing suggestion that the broch builders became allies of the Romans and upon the withdrawal of the latter from northern Scotland helped to garrison the frontier. This theory would account for the existence of a few isolated brochs in the southern uplands and in the midland valley of Scotland.

With the return of settled conditions the brochs were abandoned and new circular houses were built, often using stones from the brochs themselves. The people continued to follow an agricultural way of life.

Far less is known about the vitrified forts. They were oval or oblong in shape, their stone walls built around a framework of timber. By setting fire to the structure such high temperatures were achieved that the stone walls fused into a glass-like material, hence the name. Whether this was done intentionally by the builders or with destructive intent by invaders cannot be known with certainty.

PICTS AND SCOTS

Another tantalising puzzle of archaeology concerns the Picts, a race which inhabited the north and east of Scotland for six centuries. They are recorded in history with lists of kings, but we know very little about them. What language they spoke, what they called themselves or what happened to them when their neighbours became dominant are questions which remain unanswered.

The Picts were at first a collection of tribes speaking a Celtic dialect but by the sixth century they had become a political unit. They were descendants of the broch builders but the forts had already been abandoned by the time the name was first applied. They were mentioned frequently by Roman writers from the year AD 297 onwards as a fierce warlike tribe, a terror to Britons and Romans alike, described as painted people and shown even to modern times as naked and heavily tattooed, a backward people of the Dark Ages. In the 1950s the publication of *The Problem of the Picts* edited by F. T. Wainwright marked a turning point in Pictish studies. A more recent book, *The Picts* by Isobel Henderson, carries the study a stage further.

One of the main problems is the lack of archaeological evidence for there is not one dwelling or fort which the expert can say with certainty is Pictish. The same is true of burials but it is possible that many burials believed to be Iron Age may be Pictish. It is probable that settlement on some present village sites has been continuous for centuries and that Pictish farm houses and villages may be under the foundations of those of the present day.

There is one group of relics which is undoubtedly Pictish—the mysterious symbol stones unearthed in fields all over the northern half of Scotland. The symbols are of two kinds: animals such as bulls and snakes highly stylised yet marvellously life-like; and designs incorporating combinations of lines and crescents whose significance is entirely unknown. Some, such as the looking glass, are recognisable and some have been given a tentative name such as the 'spectacles and broken rod' but even assuming the identification to be correct, what do they mean?

While the Picts ruled the north and east of Scotland the south-west was under the control of yet another group of new-comers—the Scots from Ireland. The Scots settled in what is now Argyll to form the tiny kingdom of Dalriada and were first mentioned by Roman historians in the middle of the fourth century as barbarians raiding Roman Britain. Picts and Scots at this time had nothing in common, indeed they were often at war. In the sixth century a Pictish force defeated the Scots.

The importance of Dalriada was out of all proportion to its small size. The influence of the Scots expanded until their name was given to the whole country and their language superseded that of the Picts. At its greatest extension Gaelic was spoken in the whole of what is now Scotland, except the Borders and the northern isles.

Even more important was the Scots' religion, the Christian faith. Although Rome had failed to conquer the Highlands by the sword she succeeded with the cross and along those same roads that the retreating legions had followed home, she sent her

Christian missionaries. Christianity was introduced to Dalriada when St Columba landed at Iona from Ireland. At first he laboured among his own people and then turned his eyes on their heathen neighbours, the Picts. Along the Great Glen he travelled on his famous visit to convert King Bridei in his fortress near Inverness, a challenge in which he succeeded.

The effect on the whole Pictish nation was profound. They continued to carve their mysterious symbol stones but now included the cross among the designs. Little churches were built and dedicated to Celtic missionaries, such as the sanctuary at Applecross where Maol Rubha (the red-haired tonsured one) landed in AD 673 and spread the faith all over the western Highlands.

It could be claimed that the adoption of Christianity, the religion of the Scots, brought about an undermining of Pictish power. The Picts and Scots remained as separate peoples until Kenneth mac Alpin united them in AD 843 and founded the Celtic line of kings. The common religion may have helped to unite them but more probably it was their common fear of the Vikings. This hypothesis does not, however, explain the virtual disappearance of the Picts from history.

THE NORSEMEN

The eighth century saw an extraordinary period of exploration and plunder. The Vikings ravaged the coasts of England and Europe as far as the Mediterranean, and reached America via Greenland centuries before Columbus. In their dragon-prowed longships they sailed down both the east and west coasts of Britain, sacking the monastery of Lindisfarne in AD 793 and that of Iona in AD 802. In addition to booty they took back to Norway reports of the sheltered western seaboard of the Highlands and of the flat, fertile plains of Caithness.

In the following century when Norway was faced with the problems of political strife and a too-rapid rise in population,

Norwegians left their homes in thousands and settled in Orkney and Shetland, in Caithness, and along the west of Scotland, eventually to include the Isle of Man.

The Norse left records of their exploits in their sagas. These have to be interpreted with caution as they glorify the spectacular deeds of the Vikings and were transmitted in song and narrative for hundreds of years before being written down in the thirteenth century in Iceland. The Orkneyinga Saga relates how the earldom of Orkney sprang from the Norse earls of Möre just before AD 900. The first of the earls, Earl Sigurd, annexed Caithness to his earldom and at the peak of Norse power Earl Thorfinn the Mighty, who died in 1065, held Orkney, Shetland, the Hebrides, Caithness and a strip of territory along the north and west coasts.

Norse power in Scotland waned rapidly after the battle of Largs in 1263 and by the treaty that followed Norway renounced all claim to her former Scottish territory with the sole exception of the northern isles which she retained for another 200 years.

Evidence of Norse settlement survives in Caithness in traces of houses and pagan graves at Reay and Freswick. Ruins of several castles built in Norse times are found on headlands overlooking the North Sea, such as the castle of Old Wick.

Far more impressive than archaeological remains is the legacy of Norse place names so common in the north and west of the region. The Norse word *stathr*, or farm, is corrupted to the common suffix 'ster'—Lybster, Camster, Broubster and Shebster in Caithness. The town of Wick derives its name from the word *vik*, or bay. In the trio Embo, Skelbo and Skibo, the suffix 'bo' is a corruption of the word *bolstathr*, another name for a farm, while Sutherland itself was the *sudr* or south land of the Norsemen. The Summer Isles, however delectable they may be, were in fact the isles of the *sunn maer* or south border. Cape Wrath does not derive its name from the fury of the Atlantic but from its being the turning point of the Norse rovers as they altered course to sail down the Minch. Another interesting reminder of Norse days is the Caithness dialect which contains a wealth of old Norse words.

THE EMERGENCE OF THE CLANS

The tribal organisation of England and Wales ended in 1066 when feudalism was introduced by William the Conqueror. Gradually the new order spread through Scotland and in the twelfth century a whole succession of rulers attempted to unify and strengthen the Scottish State by imposing feudal European traditions. David I came north with a band of followers determined to spread the new Anglo-Norman system of government but under the rule of Malcolm Canmore and his queen Margaret the influx was even greater. The effect on Scotland was profound as feudalism weakened the clan system, and English began to replace the Gaelic language.

The eastern lowlands were the first to succumb to the new order; burghs such as Inverness and Dingwall were founded to encourage a new race of merchants; the parochial system was introduced with bishoprics at Ross and Caithness. Most of the Highlands, nevertheless, were excluded from these changes. To hold the new frontier, castles were built at Edindour and Dunscaith in Ross and Cromarty and at Urquhart and Inverlochy along the Great Glen. Beyond lay the territories of the Highland clans and beyond that again the land held by the Norsemen.

It is from this period of change and conflict that the clan system emerges since there is little evidence available about Celtic society before the twelfth century. Social organisation was certainly tribal and based on kinship between every free man and the head of his tribe. Land belonged to the clan as a whole and was used for the sustenance of the people, for growing crops, for grazing flocks and herds and for hunting. Under the feudal system, however, land was granted by the crown to a noble and the latter had jurisdiction over everyone and everything inside his territory.

The clan system as we first see it was a curious mixture of three elements, Celtic, Anglo-Norman and Norse. Many of the clans have pure Celtic names such as MacNab, son of the abbot, and MacIntosh, son of the Toiseach. The clan Gunn, however, traces its origin back to the earls of Orkney through one Gunni whose wife inherited estates in Orkney and Sutherland. The Frasers and Chisholms are Celtic clans who adopted the names of feudal Norman lords who made good marriages within the old society.

Greatest clan of all at this period was the Clan Donald which traces its ancestry back to Somerled who raised a revolt of his Gaelic kinsmen and recovered ancestral lands from the rule of the Norse. He built up a powerful Gaelic principality in south Argyll under the nominal sovereignty of King David I. In 1140 Somerled married Ragnhild, daughter of King Olaf the Red, which further enhanced his prestige among the Norsemen. In 1164 he met his death when he tried to invade the Central Lowlands by taking a fleet of ships up the Clyde.

During the wars of Scottish independence the Highlanders were divided, some supporting Baliol and some, Robert the Bruce. The MacDonalds were divided but Angus Og of Islay supported Bruce and for this he was rewarded by a grant of extensive lands including Morvern, Ardnamurchan and half of Lochaber. His son John of Islay achieved greater success and by 1354 had assumed the proud title of 'Lord of the Isles'. In their castle of Ardtornish John's descendants inherited the title with almost the status of a second royal house and in his poem 'Lord of the Isles', Sir Walter Scott describes the betrothal feast of Edith, Maid of Lorn, and Ronald of the Isles in 'Ardtornish on her frowning steep 'twixt cloud and ocean hung'.

The clan system became changed under feudal influence, chiefs of the late Middle Ages all holding their land under feudal charter and assuming absolute control over their tenants. The emphasis of the clan was still on ties of kinship and the chief undertook to protect his people, running a kind of welfare system for widows, orphans and the aged. In return, the people were obliged to render certain services to the chief, to assist with his harvest, to participate in hunting expeditions and, most important, to fight for him when he so demanded.

Fighting was a tradition in the Highlands, each man being armed with a broadsword on his left side, a dirk or short dagger on his right, and a short-handled axe which he used to deadly effect when he closed in on his enemy. In the fourteenth century, due to the success of the Anglo-Normans, a new distinction began to be made between the ordered and thoroughly feudalised Lowlands and the wild Gaelic-speaking Highlands. Although in theory Scotland had become one nation, there emerged the barrier between Highlander and Lowlander that was later to have such tragic consequences.

4 FROM THE STEWARTS TO VICTORIA

THE long era of the Stewart monarchs was marked by almost continuous conflict. James I, returning from prison in England, was determined to unite his country, to restore law and order and subdue the west Highland chiefs. Arriving at Inverness in 1427 he summoned the principal chiefs to meet him. Unaware of any trap they responded, forty of them were seized and put in prison and many were executed. Surprisingly, Alexander, Lord of the Isles was allowed to go free and in revenge he ravaged the crown lands north of Inverness and destroyed the Highland capital itself. The King returned and with the aid of the clans Chattan and Cameron he defeated the army of the Lord of the Isles who then remained quiet for the rest of his days.

In this troubled period the Highland chiefs were fighting both against the Lowland Scots and against the English. Both were foreign in speech, race and custom. Alliances were quickly made with one or the other as the need demanded but only to be broken as quickly as they had been forged. It was an alliance with the English against the Scottish throne that proved the undoing of the last Lord of the Isles and the title was removed in 1493.

Other clans were now freed from the dominance of the Clan Donald and were willing to make peace with James IV. His charming manners, his knowledge of Gaelic and his love of hunting made him most popular with west Highland chiefs, and the success of this reconciliation is proved by the numbers of Highlanders who were killed fighting for the Scottish crown at Flodden in 1513.

Feuding between neighbouring clans continued. In the north the great families of Gunn, Keith, Mackay, Murray and Sinclair were seldom at peace. Following the decline of the MacDonalds neighbouring clans rose in importance, especially the Campbells of Argyll, the MacKenzies and the Gordons. There are some terrible tales told of the burning to death in a church of a congregation of MacKenzies by the MacDonalds of Glengarry at Kilchrist in 1603 and of MacLeod raids on Wester Ross in which neither man, woman or child were spared. Almost every glen has its own story of chivalry or of cruelty for these were the characteristics of the Highlander at that time— loyalty to his family and friends, and hatred, even cruelty, towards his own foes and the enemies of his clan.

The church could do nothing to stop the feuding. It too was beset with controversy and marred by atrocities when men like George Wishart and Patrick Hamilton were burned to death for their beliefs. After the Reformation of 1560 the Scottish church was Protestant and free of the Church of Rome but the change was slow in the Highlands. It was easy to abolish Catholicism but not so easy to find Protestant ministers to fill the pulpits. In many places churches stood empty and in others Jesuit priests operated secretly and actually revived Catholicism. Districts such as Glengarry and Glenmoriston became Catholic in the early seventeenth century and remain largely so today.

Records of the presbyteries of Inverness and Dingwall show how little hold the Church of Scotland had in the Highlands. At Glen Urquhart in 1671 no communion service had been held for twenty-five years while in 1656 it was discovered that people in Wester Ross between Applecross and Loch Broom were worshipping the cult of St Maol Rubha with rites reminiscent of pre-Christian days. In Caithness, too, strange rites reappeared, relics of the pre-Reformation church. People visited the ruins of old chapels, walking round and round the walls calling on spirits to restore health to their relatives and to their animals.

Ministers of the reformed church had their own superstitions and between 1560 and 1707 around 400 people were killed for witchcraft in Scotland. Trials of witches were rare in the Highlands but there was a spate in Ross-shire after 1625. At a meeting of the presbytery of Caithness in 1698 it was announced that sorcerers banished from Orkney had found refuge there. Witch hunts then became fashionable and in 1718 a Margaret Gilbertson, suspected of being a witch, was killed by a mob at Thurso. The last witch to die in Scotland was condemned to death by the Sheriff depute of Dornoch in 1722.

In the dispute between Crown and Parliament in the seventeenth century the Highlands were caught up in the turmoil. The Marquis of Montrose, fighting on the side of Charles I, was opposed by an equally courageous commander, the Duke of Argyll. It was typical of the northern Highlands that the people should again be divided in their loyalties. One of Montrose's famous victories over the covenanting forces was at Inverlochy in 1645 but in his last campaign in 1650 he was defeated at Carbisdale and sent to Edinburgh for execution.

Once victorious, Cromwell sent General Monk to establish law and order and garrison troops along the Great Glen, with the building of yet another fort at Inverlochy. Then came the restoration of the Stuarts (the later spelling) and Charles II withdrew the garrisons in gratitude for the loyalty of certain clans. Finally came the Bloodless Revolution of 1688 and James VII, last of the Stuart kings, fled to France with his wife and infant son. Once more garrisons were stationed in the Highlands, the fort at Inverlochy being repaired and renamed Fort William in honour of the unpopular king.

LIVING CONDITIONS

The old tribal system became changed under feudal or Lowland influences. Under the old system chiefhood was hereditary but it was never envisaged that the prestige that went with it would ever be exploited for personal gain. Gradually the chiefs assumed complete control over their clans' territories and acts of parliament gave them greater control. An act of 1695 allowed division of the commonties and in fact paved the way for the introduction of the tacksman or middleman. Ownership of land became the status symbol that determined a man's place in society.

At the end of the seventeenth century class distinction was becoming accentuated. At the apex of the society were the great families, those of noble birth and principal Highland chiefs or lairds who acknowledged the King as immediate feudal lord. Next in line were the tacksmen, usually relatives of the chief to whom he apportioned large tracts of his estate as tenants. The tacksmen in turn let most of their land to lesser tenants but reserved fifty acres or so for their own farm. At the bottom of society were the peasants, later to become known as crofters and cottars, each having a hut and a few acres of ground sufficient to keep a few cows and two or three goats. All of them shared the common grazing of the hills which was used for the summer feeding of cattle and the year-round feeding of sheep.

It was a pleasant life for the chief, enormous quantities of food being consumed at the banquets in his mansion when he entertained important guests. The people paid for their bits of land by free labour on the chief's farm or by cutting and drying his peats. More important, they were still ready to take up arms on his behalf. The need was ever present with raids on the better farmland of the Lowlands, constant quarrelling over clan boundaries, religion, and vendettas. The basis of Highland society remained war-like in its stratification—the chief was the war lord, the tacksmen were his officers and the sub-tenants and peasants were the ordinary soldiers.

For the ordinary people life was far from pleasant. The houses were built of rough stone and roofed with thatch over a layer of turf. The design varied: in the north-west the typical house had a roof inclined inwards from all four walls, while in

83

the south-west the two end walls continued upwards into high peaked gables. The houses were divided into three compartments—the living room, the bedroom and the room where the cattle spent the winter. The floor of each room was of trodden earth, dusty and often filthy but warm underfoot. There were no windows but the roof had an opening to let out a little smoke and let in a little light. After dark the only light came from the peat fire on the central hearth and from the simple crusie that burned fish oil.

Beds evolved from simple hollows on the floor, through wooden benches to the cupboard-like box-beds whose doors could be shut tight in cold weather. Other articles of furniture were rough wooden tables, stools, and storage chests, a cooking pot suspended on a chain from rafters, a wash tub and an assortment of mugs, plates and horn spoons.

Clothing was home-made from sheep's wool, the wool being carded and spun into yarn by means of a distaff and simple spindle. The spinning wheel was an introduction of the early eighteenth century. After dyeing with natural dyes the wool was either knitted into garments or woven into cloth. The usual garment was the plaid, a long woollen cloak that served as a coat by day and could be wrapped around the wearer as a blanket by night. As early as the sixteenth century checked patterns were common, an early form of tartan. Brown was a colour commonly incorporated into the pattern since it served as a useful camouflage when hunting on the moors.

Diet was rather monotonous consisting mainly of oatmeal and bere meal baked into cakes or made into porridge. This was enlightened with a variety of salt and fresh meat and several species of fish. Potatoes were not introduced until about 1730 but kail was a common garden vegetable.

It was a life in which only the hardiest survived, and death was commonplace. In the absence of doctors healing was done by amateur apothecaries who relied on blood-letting by leeches, on their knowledge of herbs and on charms to preserve the patient from the 'evil eye'. Smallpox was first recorded in 1610 and was widespread after 1635. Crops were insufficient, the farming cycle often upset by fighting when the harvest was stolen or destroyed during raids. There were years of famine and those recorded in the 1690s and in 1709 must have been exceptionally severe.

The emphasis in the valley community was one of self-sufficiency with maintenance of artisans who could meet practically all its requirements. Timber was cut from the forests and peat was dug from the moors for fuel. Every home was armed with swords and dirks and some had pistols for the defence of the family and of the community. If it was a life of poverty it was a life of security, every person had his place in society and each was a member of a still larger family, the children of the chief.

THE REBELLIONS

The deposition of King James VII in 1688 marked the end of the old order in Scotland, the end of a dynasty that had ruled since 1371. But the people of the Highlands refused to accept it. The remoteness of their valleys and poor communications shielded them from the truth and again there was hatred of the new royal house. They were shocked by the cold premeditated massacre of Glencoe for which they blamed King William himself and their culture seemed in even greater danger when the German king George I assumed the throne. In the south-west they saw the hated Clan Campbell being encouraged by the government to keep its neighbours in check. The majority of the Highlanders remained loyal to their old traditions and to their old monarch—'the King over the water'.

When James VII died in 1701 his son was regarded by the Jacobites as the rightful King James VIII and III. In 1715 he returned to Scotland to claim his throne and the clans rallied to his cause but they dispersed after the inconclusive battle of Sheriffmuir. James, disillusioned, returned to France. Another

Jacobite attempt in 1719, helped by Spanish troops, was even less effective and was crushed at the battle of Glen Shiel in Wester Ross. But Jacobite hopes were not ended; they soared again with the birth of an heir—Prince Charles Edward Stuart. Reports of his childhood and youth were cherished by his followers; they heard of his talents, his love of music and sport; they pictured his good looks and his blue eyes. Romanticism soon gave way to the plottings of another attempt to restore the Stuarts. In 1742 Britain and France were at war and the Jacobites felt that with French help they could succeed. On 22 June 1745, Prince Charles Edward sailed from the Loire on board the frigate *Du Teillay*.

During the preceding months the Highlands were full of rumours of secret messengers from France and of the impending arrival of the Prince and his army. On 23 July the rumours became fact and the Prince landed on the island of Eriskay. From Eriskay he crossed the Minch and on 25 July arrived at Loch nan Uamh with his 'army' of seven faithful followers—'the seven men of Moidart'. For ten days he remained on board ship receiving supporters who were appalled at his obvious lack of preparation. The story is told of how they advised him to return and of how the Prince turned to Ranald MacDonald, brother of the Chief of Kinlochmoidart, for assistance. The poignant reply is still repeated, 'I will, though no other man should draw his sword'. The others, thoroughly ashamed at their doubts, made up their mind to support the Prince.

On Monday, 19 August, the Prince's standard was raised at Glenfinnan and the clansmen began to assemble—MacDonald of Morar arrived with 150 men, Cameron of Lochiel with 600, McDonnel of Keppoch with 300. On 21 August the army moved westwards, gaining support as it went. On the 23rd while his men rested Prince Charles chose the badge for his campaign, a small white rose from a bush in the garden at Fassifern which he pinned on his hat—the white cockade.

Support was not general and the northern clans in particular,

Page 89
A red deer stag
displaying a magnifi-
cent set of antlers.
Beautiful deer such
as this can be seen in
many parts of the
Highlands

Page 88 (*above*) The Falls of Shin in Sutherland where the River Shin tumbles through a tree-lined gorge. Another attraction here is the spectacle of salmon leaping upstream through the heart of the waterfall; (*below*) the Scots have long had a tradition of providing loyal fighting troops. This war memorial at Bonar Bridge, Sutherland, commemorates those who died in two world wars

the McKays and Sutherlands, were actually on the side of the government. In spite of their unpreparedness the Jacobites had some initial success and on 17 September took Edinburgh, where at the Mercat Cross the Prince's father was proclaimed King James VIII.

This success brought more recruits and the army soon numbered 5,000 men. On 1 November they set out for London, but once across the border the reality of the situation dawned on them. The English Jacobites let them down and the help promised from France did not materialise. At Derby they turned back and within three weeks were back in Scotland to win the Battle of Falkirk. The nearness of their homes made many men desert but the rest retreated northwards occupying Inverness and Fort Augustus. They attacked Fort William but it withstood the siege. In the meantime the Duke of Cumberland was moving in for the kill and the end came on 16 April 1746 at Culloden Moor near Inverness when Jacobite hopes were lost for ever.

Prince Charles left the battlefield when it was clear that the battle was lost, and fled west to the area where he had most friends. Two days after the battle he was once more within nine miles of Glenfinnan seeking food and shelter at a cottage in Glenpean. There was no ship ready to take him to safety and for the next five months he wandered as a fugitive throughout the west, a price of £30,000 on his head; but no one betrayed him—proof surely, if that is required, of how dearly he was loved. Finally on the evening of 19 September 1746 he boarded the frigate *L'Heureux* and by next morning was well on his way to France. The place of his departure is now marked by a cairn, 'the Prince's Cairn', erected in 1956. This period has provided material for several outstanding books, not least *The Prince in the Heather* by Eric Linklater.

After the Forty-Five

The people of the Highlands knew full well that the Jacobite

F

cause was dead but to make sure the British government set about delivering a lesson that the Highlanders would not quickly forget. Survivors from the battlefield of Culloden were pursued so ruthlessly that the Duke of Cumberland was given the nickname 'The Butcher'. Some wounded survivors who sought refuge in a sheep pen were locked inside and burned to death. Rebel chiefs, if caught, were exiled or beheaded; Lord Lovat fled to the hills but he was caught and carried to London on a litter (for he was over eighty years old) and executed at Tower Hill. Other chiefs hid in caves in the mountains and saw their houses plundered and burned. Although they too had a price on their heads their people brought them food for as long as nine years after the rising.

In 1747 an act was passed under which the Highlanders were forbidden to carry arms and even the tartan was regarded as a symbol of sedition. Until 1782 the people were forbidden to wear their traditional dress, including the plaid, under a penalty of 6 months' imprisonment or a fine for a first offence, and 7 years transportation for a second offence. Also in 1747 the abolition of heritable jurisdiction meant the end of the baron courts and the chiefs received a total of £152,000 as compensation for this loss of status and prestige. In 1752 the estates of those chiefs who had supported Prince Charles were annexed to the Crown.

After the period of revenge came some honest attempts to improve the plight of the Highlanders. Roads were constructed to improve communications and commissioners were appointed to administer the forfeited estates with instructions to improve agriculture and encourage the growth of new industries. English was taught in schools in place of Gaelic and the Church of Scotland and the Society (in Scotland) for Propagating Christian Knowledge, established in 1709, sought to replace Catholicism by Calvinism. English capital entered the Highlands to exploit the forests for charcoal for iron smelting. The Highlands ceased to be a 'no-go area' for the English and Lowland Scots but unfortunately the old clan consciousness was broken so completely in the process that it had to be reintroduced artificially in later years.

When it became clear that the restrictions had had their effect, they were gradually relaxed. William Pitt, the War Minister, obtained approval for the levying of Highland regiments to fight in the Seven Years War from 1756 to 1763. Soon the Highlands had accepted their place in Britain and their role in the new empire. In 1773 when James Boswell and Dr Johnson made their famous tour of the Highlands they found no trouble and little sign of feuding.

By 1815 bitterness had vanished and the Highlanders could talk openly in admiration of those who had made such a sacrifice seventy years before. It was Alexander MacDonald, tenth chieftain of Glenaladale, who decided to build a memorial at the head of Loch Shiel where Prince Charles Edward had raised his standard. Originally it took the form of a tower surrounded by a wall but in 1834 a statue was added, the figure of a kilted Highlander, which symbolises all those who died in 'the year of the Prince'.

POPULATION CHANGES

The eighteenth and nineteenth centuries saw a spectacular rise in the population of Scotland, and particularly of the Highlands —an important factor in what came to be called 'the Highland problem'. Malaria died out about 1780, inoculation against smallpox was common after 1765 and the practice of vaccination was introduced by Jenner in 1796, although prejudice against this was to continue for some years longer. The end of civil war and clan feuds also meant that many more young men survived.

The old style of pastoral economy could not support the growing population. The success of the new vegetable, the potato, certainly helped, but the trouble was that the people came to be entirely dependent on this single crop and when it failed disaster followed. About this time a surplus of Highlanders began to leave their valleys and drift towards the towns to become absorbed in the factories of the Industrial Revolution. Conditions there were often worse than those of the life from which they had escaped.

As early as 1621 Scots had undertaken colonial enterprises in Canada and towards the end of the seventeenth century large numbers settled in the English plantations of East New Jersey. In the next century the rate of emigration increased and it is estimated that between 1760 and 1783, 30,000 Highlanders emigrated to North America.

There are some heart-rending stories of hardship before emigrants reached their promised land and of near-starvation before they could support themselves. On 1 July 1773 the old leaky brig *Hector* tacked out of Loch Broom and headed west with 189 emigrants from Wester Ross and Sutherland. Many of the children died from scurvy, smallpox and dysentery, and the rest had a wet, miserable, seasick and acutely homesick passage until on 15 September they waded ashore on the coast of Nova Scotia. They had a cold, miserable winter and many more died before the first harvest could be reaped nearly a year after their arrival. On the spot where the *Hector* disembarked her passengers the town of Picton now stands. In 1973 Princess Alexandra joined the descendants of those emigrants in the town's bicentenary celebrations. Picton is not the only Canadian town to cherish its Highland traditions; there are many in which Highland societies flourish where the kilt is commonly worn and Gaelic is still spoken.

For those that remained in the Highlands the late eighteenth century was a time of bewildering change. In 1784 the exiled chiefs were allowed to return and forfeited estates were restored to their original owners or their successors. The chiefs returned full of new ideas. Many of them had spent their years of exile in London and shared the enthusiasm of Lowland landowners for the new form of land use—sheep farming. The lairds now needed cash, not payment in kind, and were not interested in the services the people used to provide. The last remaining link with the people was broken and the tacksmen were an embarrassment, standing as they did between the laird and his rents. They too were forced to join the flow of emigrants.

This was perhaps the most serious loss of all to the Highlands for many of the tacksmen were educated men and had the initiative and capital that could have started new industries. Sometimes a tacksman and his tenants emigrated en masse. The people were forced to wake up to the reality of their situation. They were as poor and distressed as they had ever been, but now they lacked the security of their former place in the family of the chief. The engineer Thomas Telford summed up the situation so well when he wrote in 1802, 'The Lairds have transferred their affection from the people to flocks of sheep'.

The Clearances

The clearances were a simple consequence of the introduction of sheep farming; flock masters needed the fertile valleys to winter their sheep and the people who lived there had to go. One of the first to evict his tenants was Sir John Sinclair who needed room to experiment and chose the district of Langwell. The former tenants were sent to break in crofts on hilly land above the cliffs at Badbea.

Although a drastic move on Sir John's part this was an honest attempt to relieve the distress of his people. He thought that the solution to the problems of the Highlands lay in sheep farming with the people resettled to work at new industries like fishing and weaving. The Countess of Sutherland also tried to improve the situation by resettling people on the coast where they could engage in fishing. In 1814 she had the port of Helmsdale constructed but unfortunately this investment came at a time when fishing was less than prosperous.

Other crofters were moved with less regard for their well-being, they were pushed to the north coast where crofting townships remain today. For some it was an improvement—those who looked to the sea for a livelihood—but others were worse off. The township of Laid on the western shores of Loch Eriboll resulted from a forcible movement of crofters from the better grasslands of north-west Sutherland.

The story of the clearances is one of the most controversial chapters in the history of the Highlands. There were cases of real cruelty as at Strathnaver where the tenants were cleared in 1814. Homes were emptied of the few belongings they housed and in some cases they were set alight even before the occupants were out. Two elderly people died as a result of their eviction and the sheriff substitute of Sutherland brought charges of arson and culpable homicide against one Patrick Sellar, but Sellar was acquitted and the sheriff substitute was dismissed from office. Strathnaver became a symbol of all the nineteenth-century resentment in the Highlands. The strath of Kildonan also had its entire population of nearly 2,000 people removed, with the exception of three families. An eyewitness recalled twenty-five houses blazing at one time and the burning continued for six days until all the buildings were reduced to ashes.

Apart from real causes of cruelty the social effect of the clearances was appalling with old people who had never left their valleys being forced to move or emigrate. It was hard on a people with such attachment to their homes and to whom it was so important to be buried beside their ancestors. The old community spirit was broken and the trust of the people in their chief destroyed forever.

The whole of the Highland region suffered from the clearances but not all at the same time. The peak period of eviction in Sutherland was from 1814 to 1819 but the peninsula of Knoydart was not cleared until 1853. By 1830 the Highlands were populated by a class of smallholders living in great poverty and entirely dependent on the success of their potato crop. There were bad harvests in 1835 and 1836 and worse ones in 1846 and 1847 when blight attacked the potatoes. Charitable funds were then opened and money came in from all over Britain and the Empire to alleviate Highland distress. The lairds too spent some of their new wealth in relief. Destitution Boards were established and roadworks began to create employment. It is interesting to note that the road from Braemore via Gruinard and Laide to Aultbea is still called 'the destitution road'. Emigration continued, the population of the Highlands was past its peak and depopulation created a problem in itself for the Highlands of the twentieth century.

A memorial to the clearances is the tower at Badbea on the Langwell estate in Caithness. The township of about a dozen houses was built by resettled people on the very edge of the cliffs. Young children had to be tethered to prevent them from falling over. It is of small wonder that the township did not survive; the people moved on, some going overseas; and the tower was built from the stones of one of the crofter's cottages.

The Highland Clearances by John Prebble tells the story of this savage period in the history of the Highlands and Iain Crichton Smith's novel *Consider the Lilies* describes the thoughts and memories of one old woman whose world suddenly collapsed around her.

5 A HUNDRED YEARS OF CHANGE

THE year of 1872 was a milestone in Scottish history, marking as it did the passing of the Education Act. Primary education became compulsory and resulted in the plain but much improved slate-roofed school buildings that still stand in all parts of the Highlands. But this attempt to improve the minds of the children also opened their eyes to the appalling conditions under which they and their parents lived. The Highlands had not kept pace with the social and economic developments in the rest of the country. The crofters laboured under the evils of the old laird-tenant relationship with no security of tenure and without even the right to pass on to their children the tenancy of their crofts.

In 1884 the extension of the right to vote gave more people a chance to make their discontent heard. A Highland Land League was formed and in 1885 and 1886 a number of Liberal MPs were returned to Parliament, but already the Tory government was beginning to examine this problem. A Royal Commission was set up in 1883 chaired by Lord Napier and it made its report in 1884. The main findings were the existence of extreme agricultural congestion, the difficulties of communication, poor housing, the problems of a fishing industry which lacked suitable boats and harbours, and the insecurity of crofting tenure.

The result was the Crofters' Holdings Acts of 1886 which have rightly been called the crofters' Magna Carta. Rents were reduced and tenancy became secure and it became obligatory for landlords to pay for improvements made to a croft by a tenant. A Crofters' Commission was appointed to administer the acts with the Scottish Land Court an integral part.

Since 1886 the British government has been the guardian of the Highlands and islands. In 1897 the Congested Districts (Scotland) Board was set up with powers to aid agriculture, fishing and rural industries. It constructed piers and roads; it supplied bulls, rams and stallions to improve the quality of the crofters' stock; it created 640 new holdings and enlarged 1,138 more. The main drawback to further improvement was that those who benefited still lacked the capital to invest in their holdings to make them realise their full potential. In 1912 the functions of both the Crofters' Commission and the Congested Districts Board were merged in the Board of Agriculture, although the Scottish Land Court retained its separate existence.

At the turn of the century many improvements could be noticed. Telegraphic communication was extended through the Highlands; the railway reached Kyle of Lochalsh in 1897, and Mallaig in 1901; subsidies were payable to improve steamer services; loans were available to fishermen for new boats and gear; and harbours were built with government grants. House improvement was given a new impetus following the security of tenure and new thatched cottages were built with proper division into a living room and a bedroom, real chimneys removed the smoke from fireplaces set in the gable walls. Those who were slightly better off began to heighten their houses by adding bedrooms upstairs under a new slate roof. None of these improvements attacked the root of the Highland problem and depopulation continued unabated.

THE WARS

In 1914 with the onset of World War I the north of Scotland became of tremendous importance. The fleet was based at Scapa Flow in Orkney and the nearest point of embarkation on the mainland was Scrabster, two miles west of Thurso. The

Cromarty Firth saw considerable activity, the village of Invergordon became a coaling centre for naval ships, with a pier carrying railway sidings, water mains and pipe lines. Three large military camps with 7,000 men were situated nearby.

Inverness was a centre for the supply of ammunition to the grand fleet and a centre for mail distribution. Spy fever rose after two German spies were arrested here early in the war and in August 1916 the whole of the country north and west of Inverness was declared a special military area into which visitors were not allowed to go without a permit.

A minefield was laid from Orkney to Norway and the work of assembling and laying the mines was carried out by American naval ratings working from bases at Inverness and at Dalmore near Invergordon. At each of these bases a distillery was requisitioned to house the staff, and for workshops and stores. Hotels were also taken over as officers' quarters or for hospitals.

The war ended and with it a period of full employment in the Highlands. The heroes returned to their crofts and to their same old problems. The glens were even more empty of people for in every district granite war memorials were erected bearing in black letters the names of those who would not return.

But the problems of peace did not occupy the minds of the Highlanders for long since the north again played its part in 1939. The flat farming land of Caithness saw the construction of several airfields, the largest of them near the county town of Wick.

At sea activity was intense on both sides of the Highlands. From Loch Ewe merchant ships sailed in convoy to America and minesweepers patrolled the approaches to Loch Broom, Loch Ewe and Gairloch. The German submarines skulked off shore, dodging around Cape Wrath waiting for British ships entering or leaving the Pentland Firth.

The scars of war remain today in the overgrown airfields, the gun emplacements at strategic headlands, and the tank traps at Sinclair's Bay that were fortunately never required. Additional tablets were set at the foot of the war memorials as a tribute to yet more men who would not return to the Highlands. At Spean Bridge is a memorial of a different kind, commemorating the commandos. It shows three commandos in full battle dress looking out over the territory in which they and their comrades trained for combat. It is pleasingly effective, the little group symbolising the loneliness of their exploits and yet their comradeship.

POST-WAR PROBLEMS

Population figures show how desperate the problems of unemployment and emigration became in the 1940s and 1950s: in 1801 the west Highland area had 9·6 per cent of Scotland's population but in 1951 only 2·3 per cent, and many communities were approaching the stage at which they could no longer exist. Only those who live in small communities know how painful the process of depopulation can be. Decline escalates; when too many people go away cargo vessels stop running on account of insufficient cargo; a decrease in the number of school children results in the removal of a certificated teacher or the closure of the school itself; old people who once managed to live contented and useful lives, with the help of younger neighbours, are forced to enter an eventide home or a hospital in the nearest town. Most depressing of all for neighbouring communities is yet another light going out in the township across the bay.

Fortunately the whole economic system of the depressed Highlands was to get a reappraisal. The government was forced to admit that previous attempts to preserve crofting were motivated by social rather than economic considerations. The Crofting Acts gave security of tenure but stopped the natural process of amalgamation into viable units; people could not make a living by crofting and no new industries were provided to create alternative employment. Although successive governments had stressed the value of the rugged crofting life the only

99

positive step taken was the introduction of an elaborate system of subsidies to bolster up an uneconomic system of agriculture.

One of the first of the new realistic studies on the problems facing the northern Highlands was *The Crofting Problem* by Adam Collier. The manuscript, being incomplete at the time of his death while mountaineering near Scourie in August 1945, was not published in book form until 1953. Still more comprehensive was the report of the West Highland Survey established in 1944 to examine scientifically the continuing 'Highland Problem'. Its director was Dr Frank Fraser Darling. The report pin-pointed the neglect of the land, the high sheep to cattle ratio, the existence of unfenced crofts in many townships, and the dereliction of crofts held by absentees or occupants who had another job.

A Commission of Enquiry was appointed in June 1951 under the chairmanship of Sir Thomas Taylor of Aberdeen University and in 1954 the Commissioners made their recommendations. A new Crofters' Commission was set up determined to get to grips with the problems of crofting, but far more important, the Highland Panel, set up by Mr Attlee's government, was considering the need for new industries in the Highlands, and already hydro-electric schemes were paving the way for industrialisation.

POWER FROM THE GLENS

The potential of Highland lochs and rivers for generating electricity was realised as long ago as 1896 when the British Aluminium Company began operations at Foyers on the eastern shore of Loch Ness. Their 500hp hydro-electric plant was the first hydro-electric installation in Britain. Although successful the idea was not repeated except by small privately operated schemes of the 1920s and 1930s.

In 1941 a committee was set up to examine the question of using water power in the Highlands for public use, and in 1942 it reported that such development was desirable and feasible. I was the late Tom Johnston who piloted the Hydro-Electric Development (Scotland) Bill through Parliament in 1943 which resulted in the setting up of the North of Scotland Hydro-Electric Board.

Johnston was a far seeing man and he insisted that the act should contain a clause to enable the new body 'to collaborate in carrying out any measures for the economic development of the North of Scotland', a clause that was to be of great importance in this area. The board had powers to sell electricity to what was then the Central Electricity Authority and it used income from that source to finance the distribution of electricity in remote areas where such provision inevitably resulted in a loss.

Planning went on during the remainder of the war and by 1950 when the Queen Mother opened the first scheme at Sloy in the south of Scotland several projects had already started in the northern Highlands. One of the first, approved in 1947, was the development of the Glen Affric–Glen Cannich area, the first stage in utilisation of the water of the River Beauly basin. The Board took great care to preserve the beauties of Glen Affric, one of the most attractive glens in Scotland. The level of Loch Affric was not altered but a dam 2,385ft long and 157ft high was built to impound Loch Mullardoch, and a smaller dam was built at Loch Benevean. A further stage in utilising the catchment area of the River Beauly is the Strathfarrar and Kilmorack scheme which provides 102,000kW of generating capacity with an annual average output of 261 million units of electricity.

The hydro-electric schemes are among the wonders of the Highlands and a tribute to the ingenuity of planner and builder alike. Catchment areas are generally small so that frequently the size has to be increased by diverting streams that naturally flow in the other direction. Although good reservoir basins are abundant, none provides an easy dam site. The valleys are wide with variable amounts of glacial debris and the underlying rocks themselves are so varied as to demand a great variety of dam designs.

Underground power stations are built where it is essential to preserve areas of great scenic beauty, that at Morar being the first underground power station in Britain. Surface stations are usually clad with local stone. Most visitors regard the dams and power stations as tourist attractions and distinctive assets to the Highlands.

The act laid down that the board 'shall have regard to the desirability of avoiding as far as possible injury to fisheries and to the stock of fish in any waters'. A great deal of time and money has gone into conserving salmon and other fish in waters under the board's control. Again this has been turned to advantage and anglers now admit that the board has actually improved their sport. Fish ladders and fish lifts help the fish to surmount dams, and traps have been constructed where salmon can be caught and stripped of their eggs for transfer to hatcheries.

Although water power production is not in itself a great employer of labour it was claimed in 1972 that, as a result of electricity being available, 650 jobs had been created and eighteen new industries established in the Highlands. For example in 1967 when the British Aluminium Company decided to establish their new smelter at Invergordon the North of Scotland Hydro-Electric Board negotiated a long term contract with the company to supply continuously 200MW of electricity.

Atomic Energy

More revolutionary still was the establishment of the first British experimental fast reactor in the Highlands, on a disused naval air station at Dounreay on the bare northern shore of Caithness. Work began in 1955 and was completed in 1958 at cost of £28·5 million. The establishment included fuel element fabrication and chemical processing plants and 3,000 men, half of them local, were employed in its construction.

Initial reaction to the project was mixed but it has proved t

be a much-needed boost to Caithness, and especially to the town
of Thurso, which has grown from a small town of 3,000 people
in 1953 to one of about 9,000 in 1973. Overall, the population
of Caithness shows a higher proportion of young people than in
Scotland as a whole—the opposite of most Highland districts.
Dounreay proved to the Highlands the benefits of new indus-
ries and showed how successfully they can be incorporated
into the Highland environment. About 2,500 people are now
employed at Dounreay, one-sixth being scientists and engineers,
another one-sixth being craftsmen whose varied skills and training bring a welcome admixture of new ideas to the northern
Highlands.

Dounreay's first reactor was the first of its type in the world
to produce electricity for public consumption. It was coupled
to the national grid on 14 October 1962, producing a modest
3MW of electricity, but nine months later it reached its design
power of 15MW and thus proved the feasibility of fast reactors
as power plants.

In 1966 approval was given for a prototype fast reactor, the
forerunner of commercial fast reactors of the future. When
completed it will supply 250MW of electricity along new high
tension transmission lines to the national grid.

Developments at Dounreay are becoming more and more
important to the nation since it is now clear that the traditional
sources of energy, coal and oil, are limited. It is interesting to
note that the northern Highlands are in the forefront of research
towards new forms of energy.

THE HIGHLANDS AND ISLANDS DEVELOPMENT BOARD

Greatest boost to the Highlands was the setting up in 1965 of
the Highlands and Islands Development Board with a Highlands and Islands Consultative Council to guide it. The board
successfully tackled problems which had dogged the area for

centuries. Instead of ushering in a new prescription for curing crofting ills it went straight to the root of the problem, namely depopulation. Crofting, the board realised, was fundamentally unstable, unless aided by income from other sources.

While the board realised the importance of agriculture and the value of fishing to communities in the far north and west, it pinned its hopes mainly on three different industries—forestry, tourism and manufacturing industries. Within a year the Highlands and Islands Development Board was on course towards its goal and its first report listed those enterprises to whom financial assistance had been given—building contractors, hauliers, motor engineers, boat builders, hoteliers, guest house owners, printers, food processors, fishermen, timber merchants, gardeners, rural craftsmen and a crofters' machinery group. The report claimed proudly: 'The firm belief we had when we took office is beginning to be proved: that the Highlanders do not lack enterprise or confidence. Given the opportunity of access to capital they are capable of assuming the initiative and making a significant contribution to their own economic destiny.'

Confident of its ability to halt emigration the board even set out to reverse the downward trend in population with its Project Counterdrift, a scheme designed to keep an up-to-date register of the skills which could be made available in the Highlands. Dounreay had already demonstrated that when the opportunity arose there was no lack of applicants for posts in the Highlands. The register included the names of people already living in the area, of those who had been forced to leave but were eager to return and of those unconnected with the Highlands who wished to seek employment there. After the first year 400 names were listed but this grew rapidly to over 9,000 by 1973.

The most exciting prospect of the late 1960s was the development of a petro-chemical complex near Invergordon to cost £5 million in its first phase. Unfortunately this did not materialise

Page 105 (above) The golden sands of Sango Bay in Sutherland, looking across the entrance of Loch Eriboll to the cliffs of Whiten Head; (below) visitors' caravans are an increasingly frequent sight in Sutherland. Here, at Durness, they stand out in strong relief against a background of crofts and bleak coastal scenery

Page 106
Lairg dam and
power station
impounding the
waters of Loch Shin

but thanks to the efforts of the Highlands and Islands Development Board several other industries were set up in the area, one of the biggest projects being the aluminium smelter at Invergordon. In 1967 the report on the Moray Firth area by the Jack Holmes planning group could talk of plans for new towns in that area and a possible rise in population to 300,000 people —a remarkable degree of optimism considering the pessimism of a few years earlier.

The stage was set for steady expansion of old industries and the introduction of new ones. Then oil was discovered in the North Sea and plans for cautious growth were thrown to the winds.

NORTH SEA OIL

When gas was discovered in the Slochteren province of Holland in 1959 no one could have foreseen the frenzy of activity that would occur at the opposite end of the North Sea. Survey vessels found interesting structures under the sea-bed, the drilling rigs proved the existence of huge oil and gas reservoirs, and names like Brent, Cormorant and Beryl became household words.

Ashore the activity was no less intense; existing ports like Aberdeen and Dundee became supply bases and the deep water of the Cromarty Firth was soon to attract industries related to the next stage of development, to bring the oil ashore. At Nigg Bay Brown & Root-Wimpey Highland Fabricators Limited built the largest graving dock in the world for the fabrication of oil production platforms. At Invergorden an Anglo-American consortium began coating steel pipes for the Forties Field. These activities are labour intensive and it is not surprising that by 1972 there was a shortage of labour in the Dingwall–Invergordon area. A bigger problem was the shortage of houses: guest houses in the area were fully booked, caravan sites mushroomed and a former Greek luxury liner, re-named *Highland*

Queen, was berthed at Nigg to house almost 400 workers. Soon a second liner was required for the expanding work force.

Along the north and west coasts various sites have attracted developers. In 1972 an American company announced its plans to build a new type of production platform at the western corner of Dunnet Bay in Caithness. Conservation groups objected strongly, claiming that the sand dunes with their rich and varied flora would suffer irreparable damage, but most people in Caithness welcomed the project. In October 1973 the Secretary of State for Scotland gave permission for the scheme to proceed but under certain conditions ensuring minimum interference with public enjoyment of the beach but by that time the company had found a better site in Eire.

The early type of production platform was made of steel but in view of the difficult conditions of the North Sea, the oil industry began to investigate other types of platform which might have advantages over steel. From Norway came a design known as 'Condeep' to be built of concrete, and planned by its originator to be built in a fjord with deep water inshore. British firms anxious to keep abreast of these developments, began to look for a fjord site on the west coast of Scotland. They found a suitable site at Port Cam on Loch Carron near the little crofting township of Drumbuie. Drumbuie lies in the heart of one of the most attractive parts of the Highlands.

There were those who welcomed the project, who pointed to the continuing depopulation of the Kyle–Plockton area, the croft houses becoming empty and then sold as summer homes they suggested that this development might save the Kyle railway line which for years had hung under the threat of closure There were others who maintained that industrial development on this scale would destroy a free and independent way of life and ruin for ever one of the most delightful parts of the west coast. What would be the effect on the tourist industry? How many visitors would want to come and see an ugly concrete tower? The residents of Drumbuie and of Plockton were more specific in that they feared that an influx of workers would mean the end of their peaceful, law-abiding and God-fearing way of life and that seven-day working would mean the end of the Highland sabbath as they knew it.

The government also realised the value of the tourist trade and the attractions of Plockton, Kyle, Balmacara and Drumbuie, but they sympathised with the construction companies who claimed that if the project did not come to Drumbuie the orders for concrete platforms would go to Norway, thus resulting in a considerable loss to British industry. In view of the growing energy crisis it was a difficult choice to have to make.

A public enquiry was held and the name Drumbuie became symbolic, in the closing months of 1973, of the dilemma that faced the Highlands. Who would have thought in 1963 when everything possible was being done to attract new industries that industrialisation would soon be regarded by many people as a threat and a danger to the Highlands?

As the enquiry dragged on the government was forced to act and early in 1974 it announced that it would purchase sites required for platform construction and would take steps to speed up planning procedures.

July 1974 marked a victory for the conservationists when the Secretary of State for Scotland announced that the Drumbuie site was not suitable for large scale industrial development but that a site on Loch Kishorn might be required.

6   COMMUNICATIONS

O NE of the reasons for the relative poverty and back-wardness of the Highlands was the difficulty of com-munications. The map shows the long sea lochs cutting deep into the heart of the country and high mountain ranges separating valley settlements. Coastal dwellers had small open boats in which they could cross the lochs in fair weather and the Great Glen itself has been used for centuries, but a journey across the Highlands was a prolonged and often dangerous experience especially in winter. Tracks were formed simply by the continuous passing of feet, skirting lochans and peat bogs and following the easiest mountain passes.

THE ROADS

The region is immortalised in song with 'The Road to the Isles', a lyric which symbolises the long distances people had to walk in the past. Many stages were encountered before the macadam roads of today were achieved and the history of road building is one of the most fascinating stories connected with the Highlands.

In the eighteenth century when the cattle trade grew in im-portance, 'drove roads' became established along which herds of cattle were driven through glens and mountain passes and con-verging on the important local fair at Muir of Ord and the larger trysts of Crieff and Falkirk. This era is covered in A. R. B. Haldane's book *The Drove Roads of Scotland*. In Suther-land the two main roads from the north-west still follow the lines of ancient drove roads, one of them from Laxford Bridge through the mountains of the Reay Forest, along Loch Shin to Lairg and Bonar Bridge where it meets the other route from Assynt and West Sutherland.

It was the Jacobite rebellions that made the British government realise how neglected the Highlands had been. In the great era of road building that ensued four names stand out—those of Wade, Caulfield, Telford and Mitchell. It has been claimed that General Wade received more credit than he deserved since many of the so-called 'Wade's roads' were in fact constructed after his death. But it was he who first saw the need for a good road network in the Highlands if only for the ease of troop movements. Between 1725 and 1736 Wade's soldiers constructed 250 miles of road and forty bridges. None of these were in the northern Highlands but one road linked Inverness and Fort William along the eastern side of Loch Ness.

More important were the military roads made by Wade's successor, William Caulfield. After serving with the Hanoverian army in 1745 he took up residence at Cradlehall near Inverness and became deputy governor of Inverness Castle, the nominal governor being the Duke of Cumberland. He engineered and personally supervised the construction of nearly 700 miles of roadworks all over the Highlands including a road from Dingwall to Poolewe via Achnasheen. Caulfield died in 1767 but the construction of military roads continued, one of them linking Glenelg barracks (built in 1722 to guard the crossing to Kylerhea in Skye) with Fort Augustus. Although regarded by local people as a big improvement, the roads were narrow, their surfaces hardly suitable for carts. Then in 1785 the upkeep of roads and bridges was handed over to civil authorities who failed to maintain even this standard.

At the turn of the century Parliament again became interested in the area and the Commission for Roads and Bridges in the Highlands was set up in 1803 with Thomas Telford as engineer. Telford was already well known in the Highlands for his work as adviser to the British Fisheries Society. He was responsible for the construction of over 900 miles of roadway and almost 1,200 bridges, most of his work being in the area north and west of the Great Glen. His roads included the Moidart road, the road between Lairg and Tongue and that from Easter Ross to Helmsdale, Wick and Thurso over the notorious granite promontory of the Ord of Caithness. They were beautifully made, generally 15ft wide except where cuttings had to be made into solid rock when a width of 12ft had to suffice. Telford spent his last years writing his memoirs and provided a marvellous insight into the social conditions of the Highlands during those troubled years. More fitting monuments to this great engineer are his bridges, many of them still in use today.

The fourth hero of the highways was Joseph Mitchell who succeeded his father as the Commission's chief inspector of roads in 1824. Much of the Commission's later work was concerned merely with upkeep of the roads and it was in the realm of railway construction that Joseph Mitchell became best known.

The development of postal services kept pace with progress in road-building. As early as 1669 there was a weekly postal service by runner from Edinburgh to Inverness via Aberdeen and by the mid-eighteenth century foot-posts ran from Inverness to Fort Augustus, Fort William, Wick, Thurso, Cromarty, Fortrose and to Loch Carron where the mail was carried by sea to Skye. The early service was probably only once a week but by 1794 there was a daily service by horse post to Inverness and three times a week to Tain. From Tain runners carried the mail over dangerous ferries and unbridged rivers to Dornoch, Wick and Thurso.

Gradually other towns became centres of mail distribution with runners operating an organised mail service to still more remote localities. A service was begun from Fort William across the Corran Ferry to the lead and zinc mines of Strontian and by Loch Eil and Glenfinnan to Arisaig where the fishing industry was showing some promise of development. Early in the nineteenth century a service began between Dingwall and Ullapool where the herring fishery was being developed.

By 1813 a horse-drawn coach carried mail and passengers from Aberdeen to Inverness and in the northern Highlands too the work of Telford made it possible for this new revolutionary form of transport to be introduced. The bridges over the rivers Conon, Beauly and Helmsdale and the great causeway of the Mound across the mouth of the River Fleet opened the way for wheeled traffic to the north. In the summer of 1819 the *Inverness Courier* could report that 'an elegant new mail coach' had started running between Inverness and Thurso leaving at 6 am and due at Thurso at 7.30 the following morning, the journey not being interrupted by a single ferry.

The mail coach was soon to have its rivals on road and rail and both driven by steam. The first journey by steam coach in this area was the remarkable one made in 1860 by the Earl of Caithness between Inverness and Wick, which took under two days. At Wick, as befitted the occasion, he was given an official reception. In his speech he stressed the cheapness of this form of travel—less than 1d per mile—and praised the performance of the coach while climbing the Ord of Caithness. Unfortunately there is no further record of the Earl's motoring activities, the steam coach did not catch on and horse-drawn vehicles continued to dominate the roads of the Highlands. The mail coach diminished in importance with the coming of the railways but it continued to provide a service from railway stations to remote country districts. At the end of the nineteenth century three mail gigs ran from Lairg across Sutherland to Inchnadamph and Lochinver, to Scourie and Durness and to Tongue, while another ran from Garve to Ullapool. Then the motor car was introduced and even Telford's roads and bridges were soon to be inadequate.

COMMUNICATIONS

The mid-nineteenth century saw a spate of railway building in the north of Scotland. By 1848 one could travel as far as Perth and in 1850 the railway reached Aberdeen. The people of Inverness were determined not to be left out, the Inverness and Nairn Railway was inaugurated to begin to push eastwards to Aberdeen and by 1855 the section to Nairn was complete. In 1858 another company, the Inverness and Aberdeen Junction Railway, completed the link to Aberdeen. The circuitous route south from Inverness was far from satisfactory and in 1863 a direct route to Perth was completed over the 1,484ft summit of the Druimuachder Pass.

The first railway north of Inverness was opened in 1862 in the Inverness and Ross-shire Railway between Inverness and Dingwall. It involved the construction of viaducts across the rivers Ness, Beauly and Conon and a swing bridge over the Caledonian Canal at Clachnaharry. Soon afterwards the company amalgamated with the Inverness and Aberdeen Junction Railway and in 1865 a further amalgamation of companies took place to found the Highland Railway.

Steady progress was maintained northwards by a series of small newly formed companies which were to merge with the Highland Railway in 1884. Invergordon was reached in 1863 and Bonar Bridge in 1864, while the Sutherland Railway carried out the work as far as Golspie but then ran into financial trouble in spite of a contribution of £15,000 from the Highland Railway. For the next extension credit must go to the Duke of Sutherland who at his own expense extended the line to Helmsdale in 1871. In the same year Parliament gave authority to the Sutherland and Caithness Railway to extend the line to Wick. This time the Ord of Caithness proved insurmountable and from Helmsdale the line had to swing westwards through Kildonan, north by Kinbrace, in a north-easterly direction to

Halkirk and finally in a wide sweep eastwards to Wick. A branch ran to Thurso from Georgemas junction. Both lines opened in 1874.

In the meantime the people of the west were not being neglected and as early as 1863 a proposal was made for a railway from Dingwall to the west coast opposite Skye. In 1865 authority was given for a line from Dingwall to Kyle of Lochalsh but owing to opposition from local landowners, especially in the Strathpeffer area, it was not completed until 1870.

Further difficulties were encountered at the western end of the line owing to the rugged nature of the country and the railway had to stop ten miles short of Kyle of Lochalsh at Strome Ferry. It was opened to passengers on 19 August 1870. On the same day steamers began to run between the new pier at Strome Ferry and Portree and Stornoway, providing a much improved service for the people of Skye and Lewis.

The Dingwall and Skye Railway merged with the Highland Railway in 1880 and in 1884 the railways of Sutherland and Caithness also joined the larger group. Later extensions made in the name of the Highland Railway were the line from Muir of Ord to Fortrose in 1894 and that from Strome Ferry to Kyle of Lochalsh in 1897. Two small companies operated by the Highland Railway, although nominally independent, were the Dornoch Light Railway, opened in 1902 with a $7\frac{3}{4}$-mile long branch to Dornoch, and the Wick and Lybster Light Railway, opened in 1903 with a $13\frac{3}{4}$-mile branch to Lybster. This was the last stretch to be added to the network of the Highland Railway.

The branch line to Kyle of Lochalsh did not have a monopoly of west-coast trade. A rival company, the North British Railway, realised the potential of the fishing grounds in the Minch and visualised large amounts of herring and white fish being carried along their rails to southern markets. In 1894 the West Highland Railway, a protegé of the North British, began operating between Glasgow and Fort William with a branch to Banavie on the Caledonian Canal. But the West Highland had no intention of stopping at Banavie—its aim was to drive on westwards to the Atlantic coast.

The West Highland Railway (Mallaig extension) Bill was promoted in January 1894 and immediately a battle began as the Highland Railway, now planning to extend its line from Strome Ferry to Kyle of Lochalsh, did not wish to have a rival at Mallaig only twenty miles further south. In the debates that followed the question of fish supplies figured prominently. Cameron of Lochiel described how large amounts of fish were dumped back into the sea because of lack of transport, while Lord Portman declared before the House of Lords that the fish landed at Mallaig were thrown back because they were too small. The Highland Railway produced several local experts who could prove that Mallaig bay would be unsuitable as a harbour. Then the proposed extension became the centre of a political storm, the Tories approving of public subsidies for transport, as the Mallaig extension required, while the Liberals opposed them. It was not until 1896 that an act was passed allowing work to proceed.

The construction of the Mallaig line is one of the most remarkable chapters in the history of Scottish communications. The engineers were Simpson & Wilson and the contractors were Robert McAlpine & Sons, both of Glasgow. The head of the latter firm was Robert McAlpine, an advocate of a new building medium known as mass concrete, and for the next five years his imagination on this project was given unlimited scope. It was a formidable task and involved 100 rock cuttings and viaducts. The spectacular viaduct at Glenfinnan used twenty-one standard spans of concrete each 50ft long. The most exacting challenge was the crossing of the Borrodale burn which McAlpine achieved with a single span 127ft long and two side spans each 20ft long. The story of the construction of the Mallaig branch and its history since its opening in 1901 is told by John Thomas in his book *The West Highland Railway*.

The railways had many difficulties to surmount. The lines

were single track and delays between Perth and Inverness added to the difficulties of operating to a schedule. In winter snow frequently blocked the line, especially in Sutherland and Caithness in spite of the erection of special snow fences. But for the people of the north and west they meant improved markets for fish and livestock, cheaper coal, a wider range of consumer goods and a quicker journey to the infirmaries of Inverness or Perth.

During World War I the railways were of extreme importance carrying thousands of servicemen to Invergordon, and Thurso for Scapa Flow. Congestion became so serious that from February 1917 to April 1919 a special naval train ran in each direction between London and Thurso every day except Sundays.

At the end of the war the first of many changes were made in an attempt to reorganise the railways. In 1923 the Highland Railway became part of the country's largest grouping, the London, Midland and Scottish Railway, while the West Highland Railway was absorbed by the London North Eastern Railway. World War II again caused a strain on the railways but the larger companies could cope more easily than could the smaller companies in the previous war.

Before the end of the war a new threat was becoming apparent—competition from the roads. The Wick and Lybster Light Railway closed in 1944, and the Strathpeffer branch line, closed to passenger traffic in 1946, was closed completely and dismantled in 1951.

With nationalisation in 1948 both the LMSR and the LNER became part of British Rail's Scottish Region. But this did not solve the problem of dwindling receipts. Passenger services were withdrawn from the Black Isle in 1951 and goods services ceased in 1960, while in the same year the Dornoch Light Railway closed completely. Even the change from steam to diesel traction could not save the small lines. Diesel locomotives began to operate in 1958 and by June 1961 the long era of steam traction was almost over.

Attempts were made to improve efficiency. The stretch between Inverness and Wick used to have forty intermediate stations (which local wits dubbed 'the thirty-nine stops'); twenty of them were closed but the journey from Wick to Inverness still takes $4\frac{3}{4}$hr. The lines to Mallaig and to Kyle of Lochalsh both seemed doomed to closure but the building of the pulp mill at Corpach saved the former and after an eleven-year fight by the people of the area the latter was reprieved in 1974.

SEA ROUTES

For centuries travellers in the northern Highlands have used ferries over narrow sounds and across sea lochs to avoid long detours. There were ferries across the Beauly, Cromarty and Dornoch firths, across Loch Eriboll and several lochs of the west. As roads became better the ferries shared in the improvements: part of Telford's work included piers for ferry boats and to the contract for the road through Moidart was added the provision of new piers at the Corran ferry across Loch Linnhe.

Some of the ferries were notorious, the Meikle Ferry across the Dornoch Firth being a great cause of anxiety to travellers to and from the north. The operator seemed more concerned with receipts than with safety and there were complaints about his boat, its sails and its steering gear. One of the worst accidents there occurred in 1809 when the boat, heavily laden, capsized during a storm and over 100 people were drowned. Then came Telford's bridge at Bonar and a dreaded part of the journey was removed.

When the first motor cars appeared they too were manhandled on to the ferries and rowed across to the other side. But the crossings were inconvenient for motorists and the long detours were now preferred, although many miles of new road had to be constructed to cater for them. The latest ferry to be discontinued was that at Strome, superseded in 1970 by the new road around the head of Loch Carron.

Several ferries still remain and include the vehicle ferries between Inverness and the Black Isle, between Corran and Ardgour, and the free ferry at Kylestrome operated by Sutherland County Council. Passenger ferries operate between Invergordon and Balblair, and between Nigg and Cromarty. In spite of continuing progress there are still wide tracts of the northern Highlands which cannot be visited by road. The only access to the north-west corner of Sutherland and the important lighthouse at Cape Wrath is by a small ferry boat across the Kyle of Durness, while the hamlets and townships of Knoydart are still served by motor boat from Mallaig. Until the new coast road is completed from Shieldaig in 1975 the easiest route to Applecross will continue to be by the ferry boat *Puffin* operating between Kyle of Lochalsh and Toscaig.

To the Isles

Crossings from the many islands have long had a recognised importance, not least the narrow sound between Kylerhea and Glenelg, the original crossing from Skye. When larger sailing packets were introduced they required better anchorages and as early as 1756 there were services once a week between Loch Carron and Skye, and between Poolewe and Stornoway.

With the coming of steamships more dependable services were established. In 1851 David Hutcheson & Company of Glasgow began a regular fortnightly (soon weekly) service between the Clyde and Stornoway calling at several islands and mainland ports in between. In 1879 the company was sold to David MacBrayne, soon to become a household name along the western seaboard.

When the railway reached Strome Ferry in 1870 the railway company began a daily service to Portree in Skye and a weekly service to Stornoway, the frequency of both being reduced in winter. In 1880 the railway company handed over its operations to MacBrayne and in 1897 steamers were transferred from Strome Ferry to Kyle of Lochalsh.

In 1833 steamships also brought a regular service to the east coast of Scotland between Leith, Aberdeen, Wick, Orkney and Shetland. It was operated by a company which in 1875 changed its name to the North of Scotland and Orkney and Shetland Steam Navigation Company. Wick was dropped from the itinerary during World War II although an unsuccessful attempt was made to revive a weekly call in 1955.

The first regular mail service between Scrabster and Stromness in Orkney was started in 1856 but was taken over by the 'North' Company in 1882. In 1892 the first *St Ola* began operating the route but was replaced in 1950 by the present holder of the name.

The link between Kyle of Lochalsh and Stornoway was for long the life-line of Lewis, operated by a succession of noble vessels. There have been memorable incidents and even tragedies, the worst occurring on New Year's morning in 1919 when the *Iolaire* was wrecked near Stornoway and 200 young men returning from the war were drowned.

From 1929 the SS *Loch Ness* operated the Stornoway run and was replaced in 1947 by the MV *Loch Seaforth* built specially for this route. In 1973 MacBrayne shifted the mainland terminal from Kyle of Lochalsh to Ullapool, the MV *Iona* soon being replaced by the MV *Clansman* which was specially adapted for her new role as a drive-on/drive-off ferry. Alterations involved cutting her in two and inserting a 30ft section amidships, which with modifications to her superstructure cost £400,000.

Kyle of Lochalsh is still important since from there MacBrayne operate vehicle ferries to Kyleakin in Skye, a service which is extremely popular with visitors in summer. Mallaig is important as the mainland terminal for the service to the islands of Eigg, Muck, Rhum and Canna, a service operated by MacBrayne's MV *Loch Arkaig*. Also from Mallaig, Bruce Watt Services provide additional runs to these islands, offer special summer excursions and undertake private hires with their smaller MV *Western Isles*. Each year the Highlands and Islands

Development Board publish a comprehensive transport time-table entitled *Getting around the Highlands and Islands* which gives details of these and other services.

The Caledonian Canal

In the eighteenth century many people became enthusiastic about the possibility of linking North Sea and Atlantic Ocean by a canal along the Great Glen, a distance of sixty miles. Twenty miles of the route were already in existence with the lochs Ness, Oich and Lochy. Ships would thereby avoid the dangerous journey through the Pentland Firth and around Cape Wrath. An added incentive was the prospect of employment at a time of great hardship in the Highlands, but the most compelling argument came when Britain was at war with France and a canal was seen as an advantage to ships of the Royal Navy.

In 1800 Telford was appointed as engineer. He proposed that the canal should have a minimum depth of 20ft to allow 32-gun frigates to pass and he estimated the cost at £350,000. It was a colossal undertaking since the surface of Loch Oich is 106ft above sea-level and twenty-nine locks were required, eight of them in a row at Banavie and popularly known as Neptune's Staircase. He had labour problems since the men hired would leave suddenly for the peat cutting, herring fishing and harvest; local landowners objected to their privacy being invaded and an unexpected difficulty was dredging Loch Oich, the remains of huge oak trees being embedded in the muddy bottom. Nevertheless, in 1818 the eastern end between Inverness and Fort Augustus was opened to traffic and in 1822 the first voyage was made between Inverness and Fort William.

Although steam boats could now operate between Glasgow and Inverness and the canal was proving a boon to fishing vessels, it did not fulfil the aims of those who had championed it. Before it was completed the threat from France had vanished, its minimum depth was progressively reduced as work proceeded to a mere 12ft, steamships were now replacing sailing vessels and lighthouses on the west coast had made that journey less hazardous. The revenue could not even cover the cost of repairs; floods in 1834 caused severe damage to its banks and in 1842 the government reluctantly undertook to carry out major repairs, a task that took five years and pushed the total cost of the canal to a figure of £1,250,000.

The canal proved its worth in two world wars but by 1948 when it was taken over by the British Transport Commission traffic was confined mainly to fishing boats. Within recent years the canal has been seen in a new light for one of its greatest assets is the marvellous scenery along its banks. Several companies now charter cabin cruisers on the canal and the pleasure trips run by the British Waterways Board's steamer *Scot II* are becoming increasingly popular. The canal still loses about £50,000 a year and as a commercial enterprise is a failure but it is a living monument to a great engineer and, who knows, it may one day play a great part in the development of the Highlands' tourist industry.

PRESENT PROBLEMS

Over most of the northern Highlands roads have improved very slowly. Under the Crofter Counties Schemes that have gone on intermittently since 1933 the narrow unsurfaced roads have been coated with tarmacadam to become the single-line roads with passing places we see today. In summer they are crowded with cars and caravans but motorists are generally courteous, sympathising with the lorry drivers who have to haul huge loads of fish out of west coast ports.

Improvements continue to realign and widen the roads to Mallaig and to Lochinver, from Scourie to Kylesku and between the Kyle of Tongue and Loch Eriboll. Everywhere there are straight new sections, parts of the old road veering off to left or right now useful as lay-bys. Hikers bemoan many of the changes when what used to be a peaceful old Highland track is

Page 123
Two great industries of Caithness—a field of oats is being cut while in the background stands the great steel dome of the experimental fast reactor at Dounreay

Page 124
The pulp and paper mill at Corpach on Loch Eil at the south end of the Great Glen. Fort William lies on the other side of Loch Linnhe below Ben Nevis, the highest mountain in Britain

now part of a new motor road. One of the most beautiful tracks in the west was that from Loch Ailort to the head of Loch Moidart, but large stretches of it were obliterated by the new road opened in 1966. It is to be hoped that some at least of the old tracks will be preserved for future generations of hikers and hill walkers.

Along with road improvements have come improved bridges. In Caithness new bridges include those at Berriedale, Latheronwheel and Reisgill near Lybster. In 1972 a new box girder bridge was opened on the A9 at Helmsdale, replacing one built by Thomas Telford. At Bonar Bridge too a new bridge over the Kyle of Sutherland was opened in December 1973. A tied bowstring steel arch, it replaced one built eighty years previously. Both bridges were designed by Crouch & Hogg of Glasgow. The first bridge on the site was built by Thomas Telford in 1811 and on a stone cairn on the eastern abutment of the new bridge, the history of all three bridges is told.

The heavy tourist traffic poses special problems for roads in the Highlands. Between 1955 and 1970 traffic in Sutherland increased at a rate of 11 per cent each year, and if this continues severe congestion will result. By 1985 it is estimated that average speeds of less than 15mph will result over 104 miles of road in Sutherland and even to achieve this the average annual expenditure will be £600,000 between 1975 and 1985.

The better roads of the eastern coastal strip are now proving inadequate for the rate of industrial development, especially since North Sea oil was discovered. Heavy traffic through Easter Ross combined with a record tourist season caused congestion at Dingwall and Alness in 1973. In the same year plans were completed for a new A9 from Perth to the Cromarty Firth consisting of a 24ft-wide single-carriageway road, but doubts were expressed as to whether this would be adequate for the traffic expected in years to come. From Inverness a new road will cross the Black Isle and bridges will carry it over the Beauly and Cromarty Firths.

H

COMMUNICATIONS

It is essential that communications are improved in the northern Highlands for the high cost of transport is one of the biggest headaches. One of the functions of the Highlands and Islands Development Board is to advise the Secretary of State for Scotland on all transport matters in their area. The board has set out a list of priorities which includes the rebuilding of Inverness airport to make it suitable for the jets to be introduced by British Airways on their Highland routes. Although the history of civil aviation in this area goes back to 1933 the Highlanders are far less air-minded than the people of the western and northern islands. However, an airstrip has been built at Durness which may be of great importance should Loch Eriboll be developed as a deep-water port.

The aim of the Highlands and Islands Development Board is to get the best possible transport network for the Highlands by integrating road, rail, sea and air communications. It stresses the need for a new system of charges for both freight and passengers so that sea links are regarded as trunk roads enabling the islands to be treated in the same way as the mainland.

7　PRIMARY INDUSTRIES

FOR a century and more after the industrialisation of the Midland valley of Scotland the Highlanders still depended on their traditional industries, especially crofting and fishing. Even today in the Highlands the proportion of people employed in the primary industries of agriculture, fishing, forestry and mining is far greater than that for Scotland as a whole. In 1969 the relative figures were 10·2 per cent and 5 per cent. The first aim of the Highlands and Islands Development Board was to revitalise the old industries and those dependent on the indigenous foundation such as fish processing and timber processing. The revitalisation of these traditional industries has played a great part in the economic revival of the northern Highlands.

AGRICULTURE

The old clan system was not conducive to good husbandry: the emphasis was on survival not on agricultural efficiency. The arable land was dotted all over with clumps of broom and gorse, undivided by wall, fence or hedge, but separated from the rough ground of the hills by a thick wall of stone known as the 'head dyke'. Inside the head dyke there was another distinction between the better land or infield and the poorer land or out-field which was not cultivated every year. Crops grown were bere (four-rowed barley) and oats sown on each patch of ground in alternate years, the cycle being broken periodically by a wasteful fallow. The fields were divided under the run-rig system into long, narrow strips, each crofter having a share of the good land and the poor. The traditional implements were the spade and cumbersome thrapple plough on the eastern side of the area, the cas chrom or foot plough on the west.

Livestock included a few sheep, four-horned like the Soay sheep from St Kilda, but the mainstay of the economy was the breeding of small black cattle—ancestors of the Highland breed of today. Every summer the cattle were driven up into the mountains to seek extra pasture, their owners living in little huts known as shielings. In autumn beasts were sold at great cattle fairs like that of Muir of Ord, and at the onset of winter others were killed for salting, while the rest had to be kept alive on an inadequate diet of straw. When spring came the surviving cattle were often so weak that they had to be carried outside for their first meal of new grass.

But even in the seventeenth century there was a distinction recognised between the rugged interior of the northern Highlands and the fertile eastern coastal strip where the people could derive a comfortable living from the land and where they counted their wealth not in cattle but in bolls of grain. Caithness was famous for the quantities of beremeal and oatmeal shipped from Thurso and Staxigoe to the western Highlands, Leith, Ireland and the Continent of Europe.

After the 1745 rebellion, commissioners, appointed to manage the forfeited estates, began to reform the agricultural system. The land was drained and improved by the application of lime; stones were removed from the fields and dry stone walls constructed. Inspired by the success of farmers in the Lothians they introduced a proper crop rotation with turnips for winter feeding of cattle, and sown grass and clover to replace the former periods of fallow. Lairds and ministers also tried to improve agriculture in their own estates and glebes. These changes demanded enclosure of the fields by walls and fences to prevent the straying of sheep and cattle and heralded the end of the old run-rig system.

Most of the area did not share in these improvements: the

run-rig system continued and there was no incentive for the crofter to experiment with rotation grass and turnips since after harvest his sheep and cattle and those of his neighbours were allowed to roam over the entire township. The main improvement here was the better price obtained for cattle, for with the coming of settled conditions drovers from the Lowlands came north and a brisk trade in cattle resulted. This trade increased in importance in the early nineteenth century and each autumn large numbers of cattle passed in droves from all parts of the Highlands for sale at Crieff and Falkirk, whence they continued across the border to England—a hard journey for both beasts and men.

The most important change at the end of the eighteenth century was the introduction of large-scale sheep farming. Unlike cattle, sheep required few people to herd them, but they required wide tracts of land and they began to encroach more and more on the common grazings of the crofters. In 1782 the first flocks of Black Face sheep were let loose in Ross and Cromarty on good grazings, hitherto understocked and in good heart. Unfortunately they were never to be so again. Before the end of the century Sir John Sinclair introduced the Cheviot breed of sheep to Caithness using the Langwell estate for his experiments. It is unlikely that he could have foreseen the outcome of his new policy of resettlement of crofters which developed into the eviction of families on a large scale all over the northern Highlands.

For some decades sheep farming was profitable but then came the inevitable impoverishment of the grazings through overstocking. Prices too began to fall due to the competition of frozen mutton from New Zealand and of wool from Australia. Sheep farming began to decline and in some places deer were found to be more profitable to the landowners. The crofters who used to tend their cattle in summer shielings were now scattered as colonists over five continents.

PRIMARY INDUSTRIES

Agriculture Today

The basic division continues between the fertile eastern Lowlands and the crofting areas of the north and west. In the fertile plain of Easter Ross, including the Black Isle, farms are large—generally 200–300 acres—and produce rotation grass, oats, barley and turnip for the feeding of large herds of Aberdeen Angus-Shorthorn cross beef cattle. There are small numbers of dairy farms near Tain, Invergordon and Dingwall; in sheltered areas below 100ft above sea-level, wheat is grown and in sandy places seed potatoes are an important crop, the northern climate being especially suitable for the production of disease-free seed. Barley is gradually replacing the more traditional oats, the agricultural returns for 1971 showing a decrease of 7,100 acres of oats with an increase of 6,700 acres of barley compared with the previous year.

Caithness is a livestock-rearing district famous for the quality of its sheep and cattle. North Country Cheviot and half-bred lambs are purchased as stores for fattening by farmers outside the Highlands area. The industrial development at Dounreay has created new markets for beef, mutton, potatoes and dairy products, milk being bottled at the Wick depot of the North of Scotland Milk Marketing Board. The North of Scotland College of Agriculture has stimulated interest in higher production from existing grasslands. An encouraging sign is the number of young people eager to take up farming and aware of the possibilities of making a decent living from farms of modest size under intensive systems of grasslands management.

Cheese making is now an important industry with factories at Wick and Tain and in 1973 a new factory opened at Inverness, set up with help from the North of Scotland Milk Marketing Board, Inverness Town Council and the Highlands and Islands Development Board. The firm produces high quality blue-veined cheese which matures for three months under strict temperature and humidity control. This is the first of this type of cheese to be made commercially in Scotland and the firm intends to market its product in all countries of the EEC. The development is welcomed by the milk marketing board since it results in a higher-priced outlet for the board's high quality milk.

Farmers' cooperatives have played a vital role in making the industry efficient. A good example is Caithness Livestock Breeders Limited of Thurso set up in 1964 to concentrate on sheep marketing. The company now holds a fuel agency, supplies animal medicines, vaccines, dips and other farm requirements and undertakes drainage contracting. In Ross and Cromarty, Easter Ross Farmers Limited specialise in the production and sale of seed potatoes. The firm's new potato storage and dressing plant can hold 1,000 tons of potatoes.

The Hill Farms

Where the Lowlands start to give way to the mountains are hill farms which base their operation on a mixture of arable farming with cattle and sheep, the proportion of sheep increasing with altitude until one reaches the large sheep farms of Sutherland and Ross and Cromarty. Here the problem of transport resulting in high costs of fertilisers and feeding stuffs is added to the other problems of soil and climate. Most of the hill farms are highly dependent on government subsidies which in 1970 accounted for 30 per cent of sheep revenues and 50 per cent of cattle revenues.

The Hill Farming Research Organisation was set up in 1954 to explore methods of improving the yields from hill farms which occupy so much of the northern Highlands. Recent years have seen a revival of interest in the old Highland breed of cattle long famous for their sturdy legs, wide nostrils, deep ribs and their remarkable longevity, often breeding until sixteen years old. When crossed with Beef Shorthorn, Aberdeen Angus, Friesian or Hereford they produce calves well suited to the rough conditions of hill farms.

Crofting

The crofters of the north and west have even more problems to face. It is difficult to define a croft or a crofter: the act of 1886 defined the crofter as a person who paid annual rent of less than £30 (later increased to £50) for his holding, but there is no clear distinction between a large croft and a small farm. Another definition, used by James Shaw Grant, Chairman of the Crofters' Commission and part-time member of the Highlands and Islands Development Board, is 'a small area of land surrounded by regulations'. One of the least understood individuals in Britain today is the crofter of the Highlands and islands, a person who prefers to live and work in an isolated community with few amenities, the only doubtful advantages being an open-air life and independence. In many cases the only source of income is the annual subsidy of £1 for each breeding ewe in the hills and the sale of wool and lambs.

In economic terms crofting does not make sense since the average unit only provides work for two days per week. Economists would like to have the crofting system rationalised,

Sketch of old croft house drawn from a photograph taken in 1937

to see the crofts amalgamate into what they consider viable units. The act of 1955 emphasised the importance of this and the Farm Structure Scheme of 1967, revised in 1970, encouraged crofters to give up their land. In December 1972 there were 18,320 registered crofts but less than 16,000 crofters indicating that some people run two or more crofts together as a unit.

The Highlands and Islands Development Board takes a different view of this part-time agriculture and the Crofters' Commission too has lately changed its attitude in realising that there is no other system of agriculture able to keep so many people in such difficult surroundings. Even if units were to be amalgamated there is no guarantee that their production would go up. In a speech in 1972 James Shaw Grant declared 'It is better to accept the part-time unit and a mixed economy than to drive out crofters in order to create sub-marginal farms and perhaps eventually a wilderness.'

The Crofters' Commission and the Highlands and Islands Development Board both realise that the answer to the crofting problem is the introduction of new industries, even those which offer only part-time employment. That is why they have done their utmost to encourage tourism and have developed a wide range of craft industries. That is why they welcome oil-related activities of the right kind and in the right place.

In spite of all its drawbacks and uncertainty crofting is an attractive kind of life. It is a life of great variety as the crofting cycle runs from the sowing and planting of springtime through summer when the peats have to be worked and the hay cut and dried, to autumn and the gathering in of food, fodder and fuel. It is a demanding life for the crofter, requiring the skills of ploughman, shepherd, stone mason, carpenter, blacksmith and boatman. His wife has to knit and bake, and care for poultry and sheep, apart from her normal range of duties as a housewife.

Within recent years a new class of young people have been taking up crofting as a career. They are not 'hippies' or 'dropouts' although they may be called either of these by people who do not understand them. In most cases they are merely people who have got tired of the rat race in the cities and are prepared to forego a job with a regular wage in return for the privilege of living and working in the Highlands and islands. During 1972 the Crofters' Commission received over 950 enquiries about crofts from people outside the crofting areas.

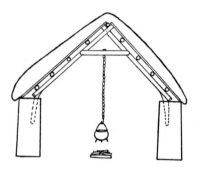

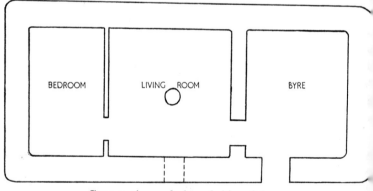

Cross-section and plan of old croft house

Under the latest crofting act, The Crofting Reform (Scotland) Bill, the crofter is now allowed either to purchase his croft or to remain as tenant but taking the title of his house, site and garden. Should the landlord decide to resume his croft for development the crofter is entitled to a half share of its development value. This has been hailed as the most significant change since 1886.

FISHING

From earliest times the people of the northern Highlands have regarded fishing as an important source of food. They are fortunate that good fishing grounds lie off both North Sea and Atlantic coasts. More important at first was the Moray Firth, a huge triangular bay enclosing over 2,000 square miles of sea, and by 1750 a considerable amount of cured fish was being exported from the many small ports between Inverness and Thurso. The fishermen caught haddock on small lines using mussels as bait, with long lines they caught cod and ling, while in river estuaries they netted salmon. Prices were very low: in 1750 in Caithness 12 haddock or 20 whiting could be bought for 1d.

Along the north and west coasts there grew a class of men, the crofter-fishermen, who derived their income from both land and sea, fishing being prosecuted from open beaches or grounds ten to fifteen miles away. The boats were small—up to 20ft long of keel—undecked and propelled by sails and oars with the long line baited with haddock or herring. Ling were caught in the deeper waters off Cape Wrath, cod being more common in the Minch. The catch was cured by salting and drying either by the fishermen themselves or by the merchants who bought them and then shipped to markets in Greenock and the continent.

The boats and gear were generally inadequate and the beaches from which the fishermen operated were easily closed by bad weather. The yield was low, the salt fish market was the cheapest possible and a typical season's catch lay between 1,000 and 2,000 ling of 5 to 10 tons in weight. The crofter-fishermen could not move to better harbours since they were tied to their crofts; indeed fishing was fitted into slack periods of the crofting cycle. Only at Gairloch did a thriving industry develop based on fishing for cod.

The railways helped the industry considerably and from its earliest days the railway from Strome Ferry was carrying cod and ling to fresh fish markets in Scotland and England. When the railway reached Mallaig this too became an important fishing port with the closure of small fishing centres such as Tarbert on Loch Nevis. But overall the white fish industry on the west coast declined. In 1879 trawling was adopted by fishermen in Aberdeenshire and in 1882 the first steam trawler began fishing. The growth of Aberdeen and its domination of fresh fish markets meant the decline of smaller ports. Another reason was the increasing popularity of herring fishing then reaching its peak along the whole east coast of Scotland.

The line fishermen from ports on the Moray Firth regarded trawling as a threat to their livelihood. When depletion of the southern North Sea made English trawlers move north agitation by local fishermen resulted in a petition signed by over 7,000 fishermen and the closure of the Moray Firth to trawlers in 1892. Foreign trawlermen regarded this as a purely local law which did not affect them and they continued to fish in the Moray Firth. For more than eighty years this anomaly persisted the Moray Firth was closed to British trawlers although Continental trawlers fished there unhindered.

The Herring Industry

There is no species of fish more unpredictable than the herring. Towns have been founded upon the herring fishery fortunes have been made by companies and individuals, but others have seen their projects end in bankruptcy simply because the herring shoals suddenly altered their migratory routes.

In the eighteenth century herring regularly entered the western sea lochs and considerable quantities were cured for export to the West Indies and Ireland. The local people had salt herring as a winter standby. When economists began to study the Highland problem they saw in herring fishing an answer to unemployment and depopulation. The British Fisheries Society was established and in 1788 it began building the town of Ullapool on Loch Broom. About the same time the herring fishery was showing signs of promise in Caithness. It was started in 1767 when two sloops began fishing out of Staxigoe. By 1795 there were 200 boats fishing from Wick and in 1808 the British Fisheries Society with Thomas Telford as engineer began to build the village of Pulteneytown on the south side of Wick bay. By 1850 there were over 500 boats fishing from Wick and the industry had spread to Helmsdale where there were 250 boats. In between, tiny ports like Sarclet, Clyth and Forse were a bustle of activity. The boats were under 30ft long, undecked and affording little shelter to their crews who shot their fleet of hempen driftnets and hauled them again by hand. The early days of the industry with its toil and hardship is described so well in Neil Gunn's novel *The Silver Darlings*.

In 1811 the entire Scottish catch was 90,000 barrels, of which 81,000 were cured on the west coast. But in 1816 the catch of the east coast equalled that of the west and from then on east coast ports forged ahead so that by 1873, when over one million barrels of herring were cured, less than 15 per cent of these were caught on the west coast. The herring now visited the western lochs far less regularly, often staying well out to sea where the local fishermen with their tiny craft could not pursue them. The fishermen of the west were still tied to the crofting system whereas a new race of east coast fishermen sprang up making fishing a full-time occupation. They invested in bigger and better craft and even visited western waters where they out-fished the crofter fishermen. Although their share of the catch declined herring fishing remained important to west coast fishermen and thousands of those who had no boats of their own travelled every summer to Caithness and Sutherland where they found employment on boats from Wick, Lybster and Helmsdale, or worked in curing yards ashore.

The herring boats of the late nineteenth century were the Fifie with vertical stem and stern posts and the Scaffie with a long rake in both stem and stern. About 1880 a new type appeared, the Zulu, characterised by a vertical stem and a long projecting stern. Although combining the best qualities of both her parents, the Zulu was still dependent on the wind and many a fine shot of herring had to be dumped into the sea as the vessel lay becalmed a few miles from port.

Before the end of the century another new type of craft appeared—the steam drifter—which made the sailing boats obsolete and forced many fishermen out of business. The steam drifters were costly to buy and expensive to operate and only the more efficient crews could acquire them, thus emphasising further the distinction between the part-time crofter-fishermen and those who were now making fishing a full-time occupation. The smaller ports declined while the industry became concentrated at Wick and Helmsdale and to a lesser extent at Ullapool and Mallaig.

World War I destroyed the European markets for salt herring but they revived when peace was restored. Then in the 1920s the industry was faced with the problems of declining catches and rising coal prices. In 1935 the Herring Industry Board was set up in an attempt to save the fishery, but the herring boom was over and World War II caused the disruption of the markets that remained.

The stir and bustle that accompanied the herring fishery is still remembered fondly by older people at Wick. They describe the spectacle of the fleet putting to sea, and the weekends when the harbour was jammed full of vessels and it was possible to walk from one side to the other by stepping across the decks of herring drifters. A society has been formed at Wick to preserve the traces that remain of the great days of the herring fishery.

138

The Fishing Industry Today

From these foundations the fisherman of today has emerged, a hard-working man who fishes full-time in a fast diesel-engined vessel between 50 and 80ft long and equipped with radio telephone, electronic aids to navigation and various devices to locate shoals of fish. His boat is versatile and can be changed quickly from herring fishing to trawling for white fish or even dredging for scallops.

The main species sought today are white fish, mainly haddock and whiting. Biggest boost to this sector of the industry was the adoption of the seine net, first by fishermen at Lossiemouth in the 1920s from where it spread to other ports on the Moray Firth and to Caithness. The seine net is still in common use but it is now being displaced by light trawls which can be operated by a smaller crew.

In recent years the emphasis has shifted from the Moray Firth to the west coast since the fish stocks of the former have become sadly depleted. There are still fishermen operating successfully from Thurso, Wick, Lybster and Helmsdale but fishermen from the thriving fishing community of Avoch in the Black Isle operate their seventeen vessels from west coast ports and return home by car each weekend. While there are small numbers of locally owned fishing vessels at Mallaig, Ullapool, Lochinver and Kinlochbervie, most of the fish landed at these ports are caught by men whose homes are on the other side of the Highlands and as far away as Buckie, Peterhead and Fraserburgh.

The Highlands and Islands Development Board is determined to encourage greater participation by west coast fishermen on their own grounds and to a great extent they found their policy on the success of fishermen from the east. In 1966 the board inaugurated fisheries development schemes whereby 305 boats costing some £3 million were added to the fleets of the Highlands and Islands. The first schemes were so successful that in 1972 another 5-year programme was started to provide assistance towards a further 40 new vessels, 100 second-hand vessels and 100 smaller vessels for shellfishing and sea angling. It is expected to cost £5 million.

The growth of fishing on the west coast is one of the most encouraging trends of recent years in the northern Highlands. The tiny port of Kinlochbervie, where in 1962 fish landings were worth £172,000, handled a catch worth £706,000 in 1972. The same story is true of Ullapool and Gairloch while at Mallaig in 1972 the catch, mainly of herring, was worth £3,243,000, putting it well ahead of its nearest rival Lochinver with a catch worth £1,114,000. Wick and Scrabster are still important with landings worth £319,000 and £353,000 respectively.

There are far fewer fishermen now than there were fifty years ago but the catch has increased greatly through increased efficiency and diversification. The Wick fisheries district which covers the coastline from Golspie around to Loch Eriboll can now boast of only 496 fishermen, including 42 crofter-fishermen, but their importance is far greater than their numbers suggest. Each man at sea causes direct employment for at least two ashore working in ship repair yards, fish processing plants and ice manufacturing plants. In these subsidiary industries too, modern methods of production have increased efficiency.

It is in the herring fishery that the most startling changes have taken place. The traditional forms of capture in the Minch were the drift net and ring net but across the North Sea in Norway a far more efficient technique developed—purse seining. Purse seining began in coastal fjords but in 1965 after the Norwegians had perfected the use of sonar to locate herring shoals at any depth, they began fishing on the British side of the North Sea. Also in 1965 a pair of Scottish vessels began trawling for herring in the Minch and their catches were so great that the crews of ringers and drifters were alarmed and refused for a time to sell their catches to any merchant who purchased trawled herring.

Inverness castle, a building of pink sandstone overlooking the River Ness. On the esplanade stands a statue in memory of Flora MacDonald

Page 142
The herring fleet discharging its catch at Ullapool. The vessels consist mainly of trawlers but the large steel vessel in the centre, the *Lunar Bow* of Peterhead (PD 118), is one of the latest purse seiners

The pressures of success soon overcame resentment and by 1969 a fleet of herring trawlers, and the first British purse seiners, fished alongside ringers and drifters in the Minch. The Scottish Sea Fisheries Statistical Tables show the relative efficiency of these different techniques. In 1972 at west coast ports drifters landed 42,000cwt, an average nightly catch of 64cwt; ringers landed 413,000cwt for an average of 125cwt; trawlers landed 1,531,000cwt to give an average catch of 198cwt; but purse seiners landed 446,182cwt for an average of 549cwt.

It is a stirring sight to see a large modern purse seiner or trawler returning to port low in the water with 100 tons or more of herring on board, but already fears are being expressed at the possible adverse effects on herring stocks of these modes of capture. There is no doubt that Norwegian purse seiners fishing to supply meal and oil factories in Norway have decimated North Sea stocks. It is important that this mistake is not repeated by British vessels in the Minch.

Fish Farming

Farming of livestock developed after trapping and hunting wild animals and it seems that the fishing industry will follow these stages too. The earlier fishermen with their drift nets and baited hooks were in fact trappers, then came the hunters with their purse seines and trawls; the next logical stage ought to be fish farming and already the first steps have been taken in the northern Highlands.

Young plaice are being bred in captivity at Ardtoe in the waters of Loch Moidart. In floating cages they are safe from predators and are fed daily by the staff of the fish farm which is run by the White Fish Authority. Even their diet is the result of intensive research and it is encouraging to find that they are growing twice as quickly as plaice do in the open sea. When only two years old they are $\frac{1}{2}$lb in weight and are of marketable size. Another sea loch, Loch Creran, is the site for a revolutionary new method of producing oysters, now a luxury food

I

although they were once an important item in the diet of working-class people. In addition to supplying mature oysters the company sells bulk supplies of oyster spawn to continental customers.

Rainbow trout are also being farmed but one of the difficulties is the problem of getting spawn guaranteed free from infection. With this in mind the Highlands and Islands Development Board are establishing a rainbow trout hatchery near Inverness to produce ova under sterile conditions.

FORESTRY

One of the most abused of all Scotland's natural resources are the forests. When man first appeared the forests covered over half the area under 3,000ft but then came the centuries of destruction. Matters came to a head during World War I when the war effort demanded the felling of all mature stands of timber and made the nation realise what a valuable national asset had been destroyed.

In 1919 the Forestry Commission was set up with two aims—the establishment of state forests and the promotion of planting and good management on private estates. The Commission is now the biggest landowner in Scotland with $1\frac{1}{4}$ million acres and it aims by the end of the century, through the extension of state and private plantations, to have over 5 million acres of woodland and to provide one-third of Britain's requirements.

The principal species planted are Sitka spruce and Lodgepole pine, both natives of the north-west coast of North America. They are more resistant to exposure and grow more quickly than do Scotland's native species of Scots pine and birch. Other species planted are Japanese larch and Douglas fir. There is some debate as to whether exotic or native species are best and it must be admitted that the long-term effects of the Scottish climate on these species are still not proved.

Much of the northern Highlands is rough and waterlogged

and must be cultivated and drained using crawler tractors and large forestry ploughs. The ploughed area must be enclosed against sheep and cattle by a 4ft-high fence or against deer by one 7ft high. Planting is done in spring on the sides of the cultivation ridges, the young trees being spaced 6ft apart along the rows which are in turn about 6ft apart. Following planting phosphate fertiliser is applied liberally by hand since growth would be impossible on the bare peat. When the trees are between 15 and 20 years old they are thinned, those removed being of a suitable thickness for fencing posts and pit props, while many of them are used for paper manufacture.

In the difficult years after World War II forestry was seen as having an important part to play in solving the economic problems of remote parts of the northern Highlands. Many districts were indeed grateful for the jobs provided, Ross and Cromarty having a total of 490 employed in forestry in 1951 while Sutherland had 166. Since then the numbers required have generally declined through the increasing use of machinery.

The area where the benefits of forestry are most marked is the southern end of the Great Glen where most employment comes from timber processing, especially the pulp mill at Corpach opened in 1966 which now employs 930 men. In October 1971 a new development was announced—a sawmill to be built at Fort William. This will be the biggest in Scotland with a capacity ultimately for 100,000 tons of sawlogs a year. The Forestry Commission have contracted to supply the mill with 50,000 tons a year for eight years from forests west of the Great Glen, the rest to come from other forests and private woodlands. In the entire Highland area in 1972 about 6,500 men were involved in forestry and its related industries, 3,500 in forestry work, 1,500 in felling and extraction and 1,500 in timber-using industries.

The true value of forestry cannot be assessed in terms of employment alone since places like Strath Conon, Glen Affric, Glen Moriston and the Black Isle with their handsome stands

145

of dark green conifers supporting a rich and varied wildlife are among the most beautiful spots in all the Highlands. Moreover, on the poor ground of this region there is no other form of land use that can provide such long-term benefits to the nation.

MINING

The history of small-scale mining operations in the northern Highlands is surprisingly long and varied, coal being mined at Brora as long ago as 1598, bog iron ore at Letterewe in 1607. Lead and zinc were discovered at Strontian in the early eighteenth century and were mined until 1872. An attempt was made to reopen the workings in 1901 but this ceased in 1904. In Caithness too there is a long history of small-scale working, copper pyrites being worked about 1760 near the Castle of Old Wick, while a vein of barytes worked during World War I near Clyth yielded almost 2,500 tons. In 1914 a mineralised vein was discovered on Achanarras Hill and produced galena, barytes, calcite and zincblende until it closed in 1919.

Greatest activity in Caithness, however, was based on the Caithness flags themselves. Quarrying began about 1825 through the efforts of Sheriff James Traill at Castletown and at the turn of the century 500 men were employed in quarries all over the county. The flagstones were shipped from Castletown, Thurso, Scrabster and Wick to all the principal towns of Britain where they were used on pavements, on station platforms and in the entrance halls of large public buildings. The industry declined after World War I due to rising labour and transport costs and the introduction of concrete pavements.

Most exciting discovery in the northern Highlands was alluvial gold found in 1868 in streams flowing from the north to join the Helmsdale river near Kildonan. In the next two years a veritable gold rush began with about 400 miners taking part and extracting gold worth at least £12,000. In 1964 geologists employed by the Geological Survey proved that there is still gold there but in amounts too small to warrant exploitation. The origin of the gold is believed to be veins of quartz and pegmatite associated with the Helmsdale granite mass.

The coal seam at Brora has been worked sporadically since 1598. It is only a yard thick and has a high ash and sulphur content but it is remarkably consistent in thickness and has a gentle inclination with little distortion. Immediately under the coal seam is a layer of bituminous shale but the richest material is under 2in thick and tests gave the low yield of 26·5gal of oil per ton. In 1961 the mine was saved from closure by a consortium of miners who took over the mine with assistance from the Highland Fund. In 1965 the Highlands and Islands Development Board financed a programme of exploratory drilling which proved that coal also exists in a fault block west of Brora. The Company ran into difficulties in 1973 apparently through the loss of their employees to oil-related industries and the mine was sold to E. E. Pritchard & Partners of Stockport.

Mining operations in the Highlands today are almost all of the opencast type and include the quarrying and crushing of stone for road metal and building purposes and the quarrying of both glacial gravels and wind-blown beach sand. Glass sand of high quality from the Cretaceous period is mined at Lochaline in Morvern. Since 1949 a specialised market has been found for Caithness flags for building and ornamental purposes.

The Highlands and Islands Development Board realises that mining may yet develop into a major industry in the area and survey work continues. Most interesting of recent discoveries are the veins of pitchblende containing uranium in Caithness.

8 OTHER INDUSTRIES

EMPLOYMENT figures published by the Scottish Office
prove how little industrialisation there is in the Highlands.
In 1969 only 12 per cent of the labour force was employed
in manufacturing industries compared with 35·6 per cent in
Scotland as a whole. On the other hand the proportion employed in the service industries (transport and communication,
distributive trades, insurance and banking, the professions,
local government, shops, hotels, etc) is much higher with 63 per
cent in the Highlands and only 43·9 per cent in Scotland as a
whole. It was in this sector that Highlanders for long had to look
for a part-time employment, thus a crofter might also be a post-
man, roadman or rural bus driver; but these jobs could not
absorb the perpetual high level of unemployment.

Even in the dark years immediately following World War II
there were businessmen like John M. Rollo, and the late Duncan Logan who tried to introduce new industries to the northern
Highlands and all over this area there were men with skills and
ideas who lacked the capital to bring their dreams to fruition.
The Highlands and Islands Development Board with its
schemes of financial assistance became the catalyst that started
a chain reaction throughout the Highlands.

The board set out to invite new firms by publicising the
attractions of the Highlands—room for development, uncon-
gested roads, cheap supplies of water and electricity, low rents
for houses and factories, quite apart from the benefits to employees—the scenic attractions and the facilities for sport and
recreation. Even the high unemployment rate was turned into

148

an asset and called somewhat euphemistically a large man-power reserve. One of the board's prime objectives was to provide modern factory space to lease to incoming industrialists and by 1972 four advance factories were ready including one at Dingwall and one at Alness. Developers were encouraged by a wide range of financial inducements including building grants of up to 45 per cent of the cost, building loans, and loans for the purchase of plant and equipment plus access to the board's own advisory services.

The area most popular with incoming industrialists is the flat land of Easter Ross. Here the local authority has set up indus-trial sites at Tain, Evanton, Alness, Dingwall and Muir of Ord and there are 2,000 acres at Invergordon zoned for development. There are now industrial sites all over the northern Highlands ranging from a large 35-acre site at Wick to small ones like the 1-acre site at Brora and $1\frac{1}{2}$ acres at Kyle of Lochalsh. It is not generally realised what a difference even a small project can make to a little Highland community. A factory employing a dozen men means that twelve families at least will not be moving from the area, while a hotel can pro-vide the part-time employment required to stabilise a crofting township, an outlet for croft produce and a market for craft-work.

TOURISM

There have been many changes in the northern Highlands since that famous pair Mr James Boswell and Dr Johnson first blazed the tourist trail in 1773. They were impressed by the scenery and hospitality but less enthusiastic about the condition of the roads and of the inns. Fortunately both were soon to be-come greatly improved through the efforts of Thomas Telford and other engineers. In 1828 Telford could write to his com-missioners: 'Along the coast of Sutherland there are commo-dious inns and at Golspie, near Dunrobin Castle there is one equal to any found in England.'

149

Along with the new wealthy middle class created by the Industrial Revolution came the first of the specialists, the geologists, naturalists, hill walkers and climbers. On the east coast where the stretches of sandy links are ideal for their sport, golf enthusiasts came to places like Dornoch and Golspie while Strathpeffer, where sulphur and chalybeate springs were discovered in the eighteenth century, became 'The Harrogate of the North'. The railways made the region more accessible and each extension was followed by a spate of hotel building.

As living standards rose throughout the present century and more time became available for leisure activities, visitors came north in increasing numbers—the ordinary sightseer, the camper, the hitch-hiker, people escaping for a few weeks from their urban surroundings. In recent years the roads in summer have become more and more congested with cars and caravans and they contain a growing number of visitors from overseas who realise that here is one of the last bits of unspoilt scenery in Europe.

There have also been attempts made to provide a wider range of activities for the visitor. Sand-yachting has been developed into a sport on the wide sandy beaches of Caithness, pony-trekking is popular in the Great Glen while sea-angling is now of major importance at west coast ports such as Plockton and Gairloch and at east coast ports such as Cromarty, Rosemarkie, Fortrose and Avoch.

Caithness is especially suitable for sea-angling, the swift flowing currents around Duncansby Head containing a great variety of fish including cod, saithe, dogfish and skate. Angling history was made here in 1966 when Commander John Woolcombe became the first person to catch a halibut with rod and line. It was only a 'tiddler' of 15lb but the implications for the sport were obvious since giants of 200lb have been caught by commercial fishermen using trawl or line—forms of capture that do not count for angling records. On the west coast Ullapool holds several Scottish records for individual species including mackerel and megrim, and it is becoming famous for its 'ton-up' skate—those over 100lb—no fewer than forty-four of them being caught here in 1971.

The Highlands and Islands Development Board has done much to develop tourism. Between 1965 and 1971 it approved more than 500 projects such as new hotels and extensions to old ones with assistance through grant and loan totalling almost £3 million, and thereby claimed the provision of 1,500 new jobs. There are still not enough hotels and one problem for visitors, especially those with young children, is the lack of indoor activities during bad weather.

To investigate these problems the government has provided finance for a research programme undertaken by the Scottish Tourist Board. The first project was done by Glasgow School of Arts' Planning Department on the area around Gairloch for which it suggested the appealing name of Tir na Mara—'the land of the sea'. Plans for improving the area include the provision of more golf courses and facilities for pony-trekking, cruising and power-boating, while a holiday centre is proposed for Gairloch itself with a new hotel complete with sports hall, swimming pool and conference room. The report was not welcomed by everyone in the area, for another dilemma is that too many facilities and too much commercialisation mean the loss of the great natural attractions of an area.

Some people prefer a strenuous holiday and the West Highland School of Adventure at Applecross offers young people 26-day courses with camping, sailing, canoeing, climbing and mountaineering. Farther north at Ardmore in Sutherland, Captain John Ridgeway's school of adventure caters for young executives wishing to develop their qualities of self-reliance through being exposed to the rigours and remoteness of the north-west.

Although accommodation is inadequate at the height of the tourist season there is a great variety available, ranging from new motels, hotels and guest houses to white-washed croft houses offering only bed and breakfast. There are Scottish Youth Hostels ranging in size from the imposing Carbisdale Castle on the Kyle of Sutherland to the modest buildings at Durness and Achmelvich. There are numerous caravan and camping sites, many of them provided by the local authorities such as the 10-acre site at Dornoch next to the beach and golf course. At Embo there is a site with first-class facilities at Grannie's Hielan' Hame, an old building made famous in song. Sites at Achmelvich, Scourie and Bettyhill are all licensed by the local authority so must provide certain minimum standards of hygiene, but under the Caravan Sites Act any crofter is entitled to have three caravans on his ground without having to apply for a licence. On these sites there are few amenities but some marvellous views and the peace and quiet that only the Highlands can provide.

Although not the complete answer to unemployment, tourism has been a tremendous boon to the area, especially in Wester Ross which had around 250,000 visitors in 1973 without taking into account those that merely passed through on their way to Skye. The main problem is that hotels and guest houses stand empty for five months of every year. So far there have been few attempts to develop winter sports, but it is possible that Ben Wyvis in Ross and Cromarty could rival the now famous winter sports complex at Aviemore.

The Highlands and Islands Development Board estimates that between $1\frac{1}{2}$ and 2 million tourists visit the board's area each year and that the annual return from the industry is between £40 million and £50 million.

DISTILLING

It is not certain who first discovered the art of distilling but it is believed that both Greeks and Celts knew the secret as long ago as the fourth century AD. From Ireland the Celts brought their knowledge to Scotland where the art developed to such an extent that all over the world 'Scotch' is regarded as a synonym for whisky. In Scotland the early distillers found all the ingredients they required—pure water from Highland burns, locally grown barley and peat whose smoke gave a characteristic flavour to the product. From these ingredients they made a spirit which they called 'uisge-beatha' meaning 'water of life', a name that has become corrupted into whisky.

For many centuries whisky was used entirely as a medicine. Even in 1695, according to Martin Martin, the people of Lewis used it only as a 'corrective' and it was not until the eighteenth century that whisky became an acceptable beverage to the Highlanders, just as the upper classes at this time found a stimulant in continental brandy and gin.

Distilling of whisky was at first practised on only a small scale, driven into remote mountain glens by the government's tax on spirits. The only exception was at Ferintosh near Dingwall where the estate of Duncan Forbes of Culloden was so wasted by government troops in 1690 that in compensation his family was given the privilege of distilling with only a nominal excise duty using grain from their own lands at Ferintosh. This privilege was removed in 1784.

The first quarter of the nineteenth century saw a boom in illicit distilling. In 1823 the government gave in and sanctioned legal distilling on payment of a licence fee and a reasonable duty. This did not immediately stop illicit whisky-making but it encouraged the setting up of distilleries to produce whisky on a large scale.

There is no secret in producing whisky, only a long tradition which continues to make the Highland product world famous. Barley contains starch and when it is subjected to heat and moisture the embryo plant turns the starch into maltose. After about two weeks the process of germination is stopped by heat from a peat kiln, the barley traditionally being spread out on a drying floor. The dried malted barley is then milled into grist which is soaked in water. The temperature is gradually raised until almost all the malt is soaked out, and the resulting liquid is then stored in huge vats. Here the yeast is added and fermentation begins, usually being completed after about thirty hours when the alcohol produced starts to inhibit the activity of the yeast. To separate the pure spirit, the fermented liquor is poured into a copper still and as it is heated whisky vapour passes up the still's narrow neck through a coiled pipe immersed in cold water inside which the vapour condenses. The weak spirit is distilled over again and only the central part of this second distillation goes into sherry casks for maturing which ideally should take twelve to fifteen years although the product may be sold legally after three years.

Besides malt whisky there is a newcomer, grain whisky, which is made mostly from imported maize; after mashing with a little malted barley it is fermented and then distilled in a *coffey* or patent still. This is a continuous process unlike the process of malt whisky distillation by batches in copper pot stills. Grain whisky is lighter in colour and chemically more pure than malt whisky but it has a less distinctive flavour. It is also much cheaper to produce, and in fact most bottled whiskies are a blend of malt and grain whiskies.

There are distilleries all over the northern Highlands: Caithness has Pulteney distillery and Sutherland has that of Brora where the famous Clynelish is made. Ross and Cromarty has six malt distilleries at Balblair near Edderton, Glenmorangie at Tain, Dalmore on the Cromarty Firth and Ben Wyvis, Teananich and Ord. There is also a huge grain distillery at Invergordon. The industry has seen many changes and many distilleries are highly mechanised. Nowadays malt may be made in drums by one man controlling hundreds of tons with a button or a switch. Stoking of the furnaces can be done automatically and with improvements of pay and other conditions, a distillery job is much sought after.

ALUMINIUM SMELTING

Aluminium smelting is one of Britain's newest industries and surprisingly it was in the heart of the Scottish Highlands that this important new process was developed. In 1894 the British Aluminium Company was formed with plans to harness the water power of the Falls of Foyers on the eastern shore of Loch Ness. The first metal was produced here in 1896 and by the turn of the century 1,000 tons were being produced each year. Demand far exceeded supply and in 1907 the company began production from a new smelter at Kinlochleven, followed in 1929 by one at Fort William. In May 1971 the company's newest smelter opened at Invergordon.

The source of the metal is a material known as bauxite, an impure form of aluminium oxide commonly found in West Africa and the Caribbean. Bauxite is first processed to produce alumina (aluminium oxide) and is then reduced to metal by the passage of an electric current; about 16,000 units of direct current electricity are required to produce one ton of aluminium from about two tons of alumina, itself first purified from four tons of bauxite.

Alumina for the Invergordon smelter comes from the Caribbean, ships docking at the company's own jetty on the Cromarty Firth. A conveyor belt carries the alumina along the 3,400ft jetty and a further 4,400ft inland to the smelter where it is stored in two large silos each holding 30,000 tons. In the reduction process the alumina has to be dissolved in a flux to allow the passing of an electric current which liberates the oxygen leaving behind the molten aluminium. The reduction cells are housed in 1,500ft-long cell rooms, the most conspicuous feature of the plant at Invergordon. Power is taken from the North of Scotland Hydro-Electric Board's section of the national grid, the current being stepped down and rectified to give the 130,000 amps of direct current required. Besides reducing the alumina the current also keeps the cell at a temperature of about 950° C which is necessary to keep the flux liquid.

The molten aluminium sinks to the bottom of the cell and is removed periodically, taken to the casting shop and formed into blocks for transfer to fabricating plants all over the UK. Invergordon smelter can produce up to 100,000 tons of aluminium per year.

PAPER MANUFACTURE

The largest industrial development in the Highlands during the 1960s was the pulp and paper mill at Corpach built between 1963 and 1966 and covering eighty acres. It was Austrian-born Dr T. H. Frankel who in 1952 first saw the possibilities of producing paper in the Highlands. He was appalled by the waste of land, with thousands of acres of land entirely unproductive but capable of growing timber for pulping.

The site chosen for this new project was Annat Point on the shores of Loch Eil which had access by road, rail and sea, a plentiful supply of fresh water pouring out of the aluminium works at Fort William, forests nearby with trees in various stages of growth and thousands of acres available for future planting. The impact on the area was considerable with local men formerly unemployed used in construction work and local firms given contracts wherever possible.

The result was Britain's first integrated pulp and paper mill where logs go in at one end and paper comes out at the other. The process here demands a mixture of one-third hard wood and two-thirds soft wood. The hard wood arrives already chipped from Canada, the ships docking at two man-made islands in the middle of Loch Eil, but the soft wood—spruce, larch, pine and fir—is grown in the Highlands and delivered to Corpach by lorry or by rail from the collecting point at Crianlarich.

After the removal of the bark the logs are passed to a chipping machine whose ten blades moving at 375rpm reduce a 10-ft log to 10,000 chips in less than one second. The wood chips accumulate in a huge pile from where they are blown through pipes to the pulp mill, for cooking in giant pressure cookers, chemicals being added to release the fibres which will later coalesce to form paper. After washing and bleaching, the mixture of fibres is spread on to a moving wire belt, which lets the excess water pass through. The mat of fibres left behind is then lifted off mechanically at the other end of the belt and is passed through a complex of rollers which wring and compress the paper, dry it and polish it to give it a smooth finish.

The industry at Corpach is hampered by high costs since Scottish forests are small and scattered, the logs having to be transported in small loads. It cannot hope to compete with paper makers in Finland and Sweden but the mill at Corpach overcomes this difficulty by producing specialised papers, those difficult to make, such as papers for maps, atlases, guide books and paperbacks. Although small by continental standards the scale of the operation is remarkable—10,000 trees are felled every day to feed the mill but for every one felled twenty are planted to ensure work for generations to come. There are now 930 jobs at a place where in 1963 there were none.

CRAFT INDUSTRIES

In the days before factory-produced goods were available the crofter had to develop a whole range of skills turning simple raw materials into articles of great importance. He learned how to build boats and fashion furniture from timber, how to make boots from cowhide or sealskin, and fashion mugs and spoons from cow's horn. The women, equally versatile, learned how to card and spin their wool and colour it with natural dyes before knitting garments or weaving tweed. These skills have been developed into the variety of craft industries we have today.

The Highlands and Islands Development Board, aware of this potential, offered practical help and financial assistance to people in crofting communities to help them develop old skills and learn new ones. Already training has been given in leather working, boat building, sheep-skin curing, stone polishing, silversmithing, pottery and wood turning.

From being a part-time ancillary to crofting, however, craft work has quickly developed into a full-time pursuit in small factories all over the Highlands. There is a ready demand from tourists since genuine hand-made articles like purses in deerskin are much superior to the cheap foreign-made souvenirs that used to dominate the tourist market. Especially popular are hand-woven articles such as blankets, travel rugs, scarves and headsquares and in many places there is the added attraction of seeing them being produced.

There is a steady demand for ornaments made from polished stone. There is a wide range of semi-precious stones in the northern Highlands such as cornelian, jasper and chalcedony which can make very attractive jewellery. Serpentine is easily worked into ashtrays, penholders, bases for cigarette lighters or ornaments merely symbolic of the rugged nature of the Highlands. Pottery has been introduced at many places and one of the attractions at John o' Groats is a local potter working at his wheel. At Balnakiel near Durness there is a remarkable craft village (an old camp no longer required by the Ministry of Defence) where several families now reside engaged in pottery, weaving, woodwork, metalwork and stone polishing.

One of the most unusual of crafts is that practised at John o' Groats where the locally found 'groatie buckies' (tiny cowrie shells) are pierced to make necklaces. They are also incorporated with polished pebbles in jewellery. The latest addition to the range is the remarkably life-like mouse whose body is a horse whelk with cowries for ears. This is probably the oldest craft still surviving in Scotland for cowrie necklaces have been found in a 6,000-year-old Middle-Stone-Age site at Oronsay in the Inner Hebrides.

Caithness has also seen the birth of the Highlands' newest

Page 159
Crofts at Loch
Torridon, Ross and
Cromarty—a scene
typical of most of the
northern Highlands
with small patches of
arable land sand-
wiched between the
rugged hills and the
sea

Page 160 (*above*) Ullapool in Wester Ross—a well planned fishing village laid out in 1789. It is popular with visitors as is indicated by the numerous hotels and the large caravan site on the promontory. Alongside the quay the roll-on/roll-off motor vessel *Clansman* prepares for her crossing to Stornoway; (*below*) Rosemarkie, typical of the many small towns on the well favoured east coast

craft industry—glass blowing—which was started in a factory at Wick in 1960. Technologists, designers and glass blowers were brought from various glass-blowing centres in Europe to train local apprentices and by 1972 the labour force totalled ninety including five engravers who use the fifteenth-century method of glass engraving. Caithness glass is now recognised as the best of modern artistic glassware, its reputation being boosted recently when several trophies awarded to winners of TV competitions have carried the now famous trademark—CG.

MISCELLANEOUS

The woollen industry has a long history in this area having developed from the primitive methods of carding and spinning by hand. Inverness has long been its centre, the Holm Woollen Mills of James Pringle Limited being founded as long ago as 1780. This was originally a small country mill driven by water power but on the invention of the Spinning Jenny this apparatus was installed. Today the mill is staffed by skilled technicians and employees operating the latest types of machinery but the quality is not impaired and the firm produces a wide range of woollen garments and tweeds. Another long-established firm is that of T. M. Hunter Limited at Brora which took over a disused mill in 1901 and since then has seen the labour force increase to 120 in 1973.

For generations throughout the Highlands and islands, the names Pringle and Hunter have been synonymous with high quality yarns. The wives of Shetland's crofters send their wool to be spun into the soft yarn upon which their home knitting industry is based; from Orkney and all parts of the Highlands wool is sent by rail, road and boat for conversion into blankets, tweeds and bed covers. These operations are in addition to the mills' main business of producing articles for their own home and export markets.

In 1785 David Dale and others attempted to introduce cotton

K   161

spinning at Spinningdale beside the Dornoch Firth in Sutherland. This attempt to introduce a new industry at a time of
great distress ended when the building was unfortunately
gutted by fire in 1809. All that now remains is the burned-out
shell.

Boat building is a traditional industry in the northern Highlands and small wooden fishing boats and pleasure craft are
still produced by yards at Wick and Invergordon. Wood no
longer has a monopoly of this industry and with the backing
of the Highlands and Islands Development Board and Thurso
Town Council, Scotland's first ferro-cement boat builder is in
operation at Scrabster. A frame of steel mesh is plastered with
cement which actually increases in strength as it gets older. One
of the main advantages of this material over wood is the low
cost of maintenance, there being no need to haul the vessel
ashore for painting every year.

Oil-related Industries

The extraction of oil from the sea-bed takes place in three
stages—the exploration phase, the production stage and the
subsequent history of oil after it reaches the shore. The exploration phase brought activity to established ports like Montrose,
Aberdeen, Peterhead and Lerwick; it was the production stage
that first made an impact on the northern Highlands, especially
the construction of production platforms.

An oil platform is entirely different from an oil rig. The latter
is a movable piece of equipment used in finding undersea oil-
fields; a production platform is a much larger structure used to
extract the oil from its reservoir. The platform rests on the sea
floor and it is essential to have the working deck well clear of the
waves. Considering that the Forties Field lies under 400ft of
water it is obvious that a colossal structure will be required.

First development took place at Nigg Bay in the Cromarty
Firth where on a 180-acre site Brown & Root-Wimpey Highland
Fabricators Limited built the biggest graving dock in the world

at a cost of £18 million for the construction of steel production platforms. Construction of the dock began in February 1972 and work on the first order—a jacket section for British Petroleum—began on 21 September 1972. When the 460ft high section was completed the dock was flooded and the section towed to its location on the Forties Field and fastened with piles to the sea floor. The work force includes a high proportion of specially trained welders and reached a total of 1,700 at the end of 1973.

On account of the high cost of steel and the increasing size of platforms as oil reserves are found in deeper water, the industry has had to consider other forms of construction. Two alternatives presented themselves—concrete platforms and a hybrid concrete-steel type. These are built in the vertical, towed out in the same position and rest under their own weight without the need for piling them to the sea floor.

To bring the oil ashore from the Forties Field a pipeline was laid to Cruden Bay near Peterhead. At the Invergordon works of MK-Shand Limited, an Anglo-American consortium, the pipes were coated with a protective mixture that included coal tar, fibreglass, iron ore and cement. In November 1973 the company announced a £9 million contract from Total Oil Marine for the coating of 230 miles of pipeline to take gas from the Frigg field to the landfall at St Fergus. The firm had previously been awarded the contract for coating the pipes to take the gas from St Fergus to England.

The third stage of oil production includes such projects as marine terminals capable of handling giant tankers, oil storage facilities and refineries. These projects demand deep water and one of the places best suited for them is again the Cromarty Firth. In view of the intense industrial activity expected, a port authority was set up on 1 January 1974, being responsible for the whole of the Cromarty Firth from Findon and Ardullie to the open sea, and including existing ports of Invergordon and Cromarty as well as sites at Alness, Evanton and Nigg Bay. It

163

will control and promote harbour development and will have power to carry out dredging: no one else will be allowed to do so without a licence from the authority. It will have powers to safeguard the environment and the reclamation areas at Nigg Bay are designed to have as little interference as possible with the feeding grounds of many species of aquatic birds.

The scale of oil-related activities is far greater than anything the northern Highlands have ever seen. Since World War II new industries have been lured into selected areas to absorb pockets of unemployment; they were generally small projects and a factory employing a few scores of people was considered large. An oil project is less selective—it dictates the kind of natural conditions it must have and once started it may count its labour force in hundreds if not in thousands. What is more it must get its workers even if it has to compete with other concerns and draw off workers from other industries—even those once regarded as so vital to the economy of the Highlands.

It is important that we should learn from the mistakes of the past and prevent the sacrifice of natural amenities for short-term gain. On the other hand it is wise to remember the appalling record of poverty, unemployment and depopulation that has characterised the Highlands for the last two centuries and is still more than just a memory. Oil is now part of the Highlands and it is bringing with it a wide range of subsidiary industries to diversify the economy. Perhaps these developments will for the first time stop the export of educated young men and women who could play such an important part in their own communities.

9   INVERNESS

INVERNESS occupies a unique position in a green hollow
at the north-eastern end of the Great Glen, almost surrounded
by rings of mountains and hills except on its eastern flank
which is open to the Moray Firth. From the Castlehill is a
breathtaking view that condenses all the varied features of the
Highlands. To the north-west across the Beauly Firth rises the
bulk of Ben Wyvis; to the south-west runs the Great Glen with
its patches of dark green forest, its patterned fields and glimpses
of shining water; to the south-east is a vista of fertile farms and
heather moorland stretching away towards Daviot; while below
the swift-flowing River Ness cuts through the old town of red
sandstone buildings that the Celts so long ago named Inver (the
mouth of) Ness.

The town is sheltered by mountains from the westerly and
south-westerly winds that account for two-thirds of the annual
readings; sunshine amounts are high with an average of 1,256hr
per year; rainfall is low with around 26in a year and average
temperatures are such as one would expect for lower latitudes
of Britain.

Inverness is the gateway to the northern Highlands with road
and rail links to the Cromarty Firth and on to Sutherland and
Caithness, while from the airport of Dalcross air links are
maintained with Wick, Orkney, Shetland and the Outer
Hebrides. The population of Inverness is around 35,000 but it
has a much greater importance than its size suggests since there
are no larger towns to the north or west while in other directions
the nearest towns of greater size are Aberdeen, Perth and the
industrial towns of Clydeside.

HISTORY

The land at the head of the Great Glen is one of the oldest inhabited parts of Scotland with archaeological finds dating back to Stone Age times. The first written reference to a settlement here is to be found in Adamnan's Life of St Columba, for in the sixth century AD St Columba travelled north to visit King Bridei in his fortress beside the River Ness. Adamnan is vague about its exact location but many believe it must have stood on the summit of Craig Phadrig, a 556ft hill west of the river, where there are traces of an even older vitrified fort.

The next castle at Inverness stood on high ground to the east of the present Castlehill and here King Duncan was slain by Macbeth in 1040, the event being immortalised by Shakespeare in *Macbeth*. It was not until the time of King David I (1124–1153) that the first stone-walled fortress was built on the present Castlehill and under its protection the little town developed. King David I made it a royal burgh and appointed a sheriff with responsibility for law and order in the region to the north or as much as was controlled by the Anglo-Norman lords. The town acquired a reputation as a trading centre, exporting hides, skins, wool and furs to the Baltic and Mediterranean countries and William the Lion (1165–1214) recognised its growing importance and granted four charters, the first dating from 1180.

During the war for Scottish independence Highland support for Sir William Wallace and King Robert the Bruce was organised here and the castle itself was held for a time by the English. When independence from England was assured, Scottish kings came to regard Inverness in a different light— the centre from which they tried to control unruly Highland chiefs. Inverness became a frontier town and time and again it was besieged by clansmen and burned to the ground.

Violence continued during the reign of Mary Queen of Scots

who visited Inverness in 1562 but was refused entry to the castle by its governor Alexander Gordon. A week later the castle was stormed and six rebels including Alexander Gordon were hanged from its walls. In the following century Inverness became the headquarters of the covenanting forces and for this reason suffered the wrath of the Marquis of Montrose. He passed through the town in triumph on his way to devastate the country of the Frasers who were loyal to the Covenant and he passed through the town again after his final defeat at Carbisdale. This time he was a prisoner on his way to Edinburgh for his trial and subsequent execution. It is recorded that an old woman screamed at him as he passed, telling him to look at the ruins of her house which his soldiers had burned on his previous visit. One of the last acts of kindness he received was when he passed the town cross and the magistrates standing there offered him a drink of wine to refresh him.

The strategic importance of Inverness was clear to Oliver Cromwell whose forces occupied the town in 1651. Cromwell planned and constructed a mighty fortress in the shape of a regular pentagon with three-pointed bastions at each corner. Work began in 1652 at the chosen site on the east side of the Ness on an isthmus almost surrounded by marshes. For added protection the only landward link was cut by a flat-bottomed ditch and crossed by a timber bridge leading to a heavy drawbridge. In the centre of the fortress stood a great stone building housing on successive floors a magazine, granary and church. The fortress cost £80,000 to build—an enormous sum in the seventeenth century.

According to contemporary reports there was considerable admiration for the English soldiers and English goods, one writer claiming that 'they not only civilised but enriched the place'. In 1729 a writer maintained that the people spoke as good English as those in London and that since Cromwell's time the people were in manner and dress entirely English. Modern authorities doubt whether this theory is correct but whatever the reason the people of Inverness are still regarded as speaking the purest, most accent-free English of the entire British Isles.

'Oliver's fort' did not survive long as the minister of Kirkhill foretold at the time of its construction. He predicted that it would not stand since it was a 'sacrilegious structure' having been built with stones from Kinloss Abbey, Beauly Priory, St Mary's Church and other churches. His forecast was correct for on the restoration of King Charles II in 1661 the fortress was demolished and its stones in turn were taken to construct other buildings. The only surviving fragment of the great pentagon is a small clock tower that stands just off Shore Street.

For many years the River Ness had been crossed by a wooden bridge but this collapsed in 1664 and was not replaced until 21 years later. A sum of money was raised by voluntary subscription from all over Scotland and a new bridge of seven arches was built, the first stone bridge in the Highlands.

A new era of improvement seemed to be dawning for Inverness. In 1669 a weekly post was established with Edinburgh via Aberdeen; in 1668 money for an alms house for the town's poor was given by Provost Alexander Dunbar; early in the eighteenth century the town's streets were paved with flagstones; and a Town House was built complete with a reading room on the ground floor. Trade was increasing, the merchants becoming wealthy as their ships sailed with meal, beef, wool and cured fish and returned from the Low Countries and France with wines, books, silverware, velvet and silks indicating a life of genteel refinement, at least for the merchants and clan chiefs. Then the whole town was caught up in the intrigue, drama and tragic aftermath of the Jacobite rebellions.

The people of Inverness were divided in their loyalties. As the sheriff, Sir Robert Munro, read the proclamation of King George I in 1714 there were shouts of 'God save King James'. Supporters of the House of Hanover celebrated by placing lighted candles in their windows that night, but the town magistrates, loyal to the Stuarts, invited a group of Jacobites to go and smash the windows of the Hanoverian sympathisers. The lairds were equally divided; there was Duncan Forbes of Culloden, who did more than any other to restrain Jacobite chiefs from taking up arms, and there was William McIntosh, laird of Borlum, who did more than any other to encourage them. Borlum was taken prisoner at Preston in 1715 but he made a daring escape from Newgate prison and made his way to France. He fought for the Stuarts in 1719 but was captured again and imprisoned in Edinburgh until his death in 1743.

In the 1715 rebellion the castle was taken by the Jacobites but was recaptured by General Wade who rebuilt it and renamed it 'Fort George' in honour of the King. In the 1745 rebellion Inverness saw much more activity but not until the closing stages of the campaign. The town was garrisoned for the government by the Earl of Loudon with a force made up in part of northern clansmen, including Gunns, Munros and MacKays and a company raised in Inverness itself. On 18 February 1746 after his long retreat from England, Prince Charles entered Inverness and laid siege to Fort George which surrendered two days later and was ignominiously blown up.

For almost two months the Prince and his army stayed in the neighbourhood of Inverness, the social life of the town being enlightened by numerous balls and parties. It was recorded that the Prince was always in high spirits—he could not have foreseen the cruel death that awaited so many of his supporters on 16 April at Culloden Moor a few miles east of the town. The site of the battle, with such poignant reminders as the graves of the clans and 'the well of the dead', is now preserved for the nation by the National Trust for Scotland. A small thatched house known as Old Leanach Cottage has been restored almost as it was when the opposing forces fought the battle around it.

Inverness tasted of the aftermath of Culloden when the Hanoverian army took its revenge. Homes were ransacked, churches turned into prisons, the town hall was taken over as

army headquarters and prisoners were shot in the parish churchyard. The policy of 'pacification' by murder, fire and pillage
was extended to the surrounding districts of Glen Moriston,
Glen Urquhart and the Chisholm country of Strathglass, areas
which had given the Prince a measure of support. Frustration
fanned the flame of hatred, for in spite of all their efforts the
soldiers could not capture the fugitive. The Duke of Cumberland is remembered for two reasons in Inverness: for his cruelty
and for having the streets cleaned. Perhaps 'the butcher' should
be renamed 'the founder of Inverness Town Cleansing Department'!

The nineteenth century saw many different improvements in
Inverness; in 1803 the Northern Infirmary was opened, soon to
be of great service to the whole of the northern Highlands; in
1817 the town became the centre of the Highlands' wool and
sheep trade and in 1826 the streets were lit by gas. The building
of the present castle began in 1834 on the site of Fort George,
while the Town House, the building in Gothic style that stands
in the High Street, was built between 1878 and 1882. In the
council chamber is a framed document bearing the signatures of
the cabinet ministers who met here under Prime Minister Lloyd
George in 1921 when his Highland holiday was interrupted to
consider Irish problems. This was the first time that a cabinet
meeting had been held outside London.

In front of the town hall stands a relic of old Inverness—the
town cross where traitors were denounced and where in more
settled times merchants transacted their business. Embedded
in the ground lies a curious lozenge-shaped stone known as
clach-na-cuddain—'the stone of the tubs'. The name derives
from the days before Inverness had a piped water supply, when
women had to carry water from the river. On their way home
they would stop at the stone for a rest and a chat with the other
women. This spot continued to be a meeting place and the stone
is so dear to Invernessians that exiles all over the world call
themselves 'Clachnacuddin boys' while one of the town's three

170

football teams playing in the Highland League is called Clach-nacuddin.

Communications

The greatest improvements of the nineteenth century were communications with the south. In 1828 a petition to the government pointed out the deplorable delays in mail delivery, mainly caused by the fact that although a regular service for passengers had been running by four-horse coach from Perth since 1809, the mail was still carried on the circuitous road via Aberdeen. In 1836 all protests were silenced by the introduction of a daily mail and passenger coach operating between Perth and Inverness over the Highland road.

Most ambitious scheme of all in the nineteenth century was the construction of the Caledonian canal. By September 1819 it was possible to travel from Inverness to Fort Augustus by canal and loch and in November 1820 Henry Bell established a service by steamer between Muirtown Locks, Inverness and Fort Augustus. The *Stirling Castle* was only 68ft long and powered by an 18hp engine but she was important to the people of Inverness as an example of improvements to come. Finally in October 1822 the whole canal was navigable between Inverness and Fort William and three steamers were put into operation between Glasgow and Inverness, the return journey taking six days.

Passenger traffic increased steadily and in the summer of 1863 over 15,000 people travelled through the canal. In 1866 the famous paddle steamer *Gondolier*, specially designed for service on the canal, began running between Inverness and Banavie and seven years later carried her most important passenger, Queen Victoria. There was fierce competition between the various companies that operated vessels on the canal but gradually the traffic between Glasgow and Inverness was absorbed by David MacBrayne who now had a virtual monopoly on the west coast.

The opening of the railway between Perth and Inverness in 1863 was a blow to passenger traffic on the canal, but this was offset to some extent with the opening of the West Highland Railway's branch line to Banavie in 1895. In 1919 the canal was transferred to the newly established Ministry of Transport but it failed to recapture its pre-war passenger and goods traffic which was now carried by the railways.

The old *Gondolier* suffered an ignominious end. After a long active life she left the canal service in 1939 and was taken over by the Admiralty. She was stripped of all her fittings and towed to Scapa Flow in Orkney where she was scuttled to block a channel after the sinking of the *Royal Oak* had highlighted a weakness in the Flow's defence. It was an ironic end for a vessel which had spent her entire life on an inland waterway.

An Inverness firm that symbolises the development of communications in the north is MacRae & Dick which started in 1878 when Mr Roderick MacRae, postmaster and horse hirer in Beauly and Mr William Dick of Redcastle, opened a hiring establishment in the Highland capital. This firm soon had strong links with gentlemen in Caithness and Sutherland and at one time it had no fewer than 300 horses in its stables and operated gigs, landaus, phaetons and dog carts.

As the popularity of the motor car increased this became the firm's main interest. Every aspect of motoring was catered for, the firm acting as motor agents, engineers, hirers and haulage contractors while its passenger services operated within a wide radius of Inverness. The road haulage section was acquired by the London, Midland and Scottish Railway in 1936 while the passenger services were taken over by Scottish Omnibuses Limited and incorporated into Highland Omnibuses Limited on 1 November 1958.

When the potential of air travel was realised, MacRae & Dick in 1933 pioneered air services to Wick and Orkney with their subsidiary company, Highland Airways, the first internal airline to be awarded a mail contract by the GPO. This company was later absorbed in Scottish Airways and in 1947 became part of the nationalised British European Airways.

Today MacRae & Dick has branches in Dingwall, Fort William, Tain, Wick and Thurso and employs 350 people. The headquarters is still in Academy Street, Inverness, on a site acquired by the original partners in 1895.

INVERNESS TODAY

By English standards Inverness is only a small town but the size and quality of its centre reveal its importance as the market town—the centre of commerce and entertainment for a wide area. It is also an administrative centre housing a wide range of local and central government departments including the Forestry Commission (North Conservancy), the Northern Regional Hospital Board, the North of Scotland Milk Marketing Board and the Department of Agriculture and Fisheries for Scotland (Highland Area). From Inverness the Crofters' Commission keeps a watchful eye on the crofting areas and their problems and here the Highlands and Islands Development Board formulated the plans that have brought new life to the whole Highland area.

Inverness itself has shared in the improved economic situation and has seen an increase in its population from 29,508 in 1961 to 34,670 in 1971. It has a variety of industries old and new including such traditional activities as distilling, boat building, craft industries and the manufacture of woollen goods. New industries are concentrated on delta flats north of the town known as the Longman; here a light industrial estate has been set up with 89 acres zoned for development. It has easy access to both the railway and the harbour. New industries include the manufacture of automatic welding machines for use in motor car, shipbuilding and steel industries, while Tarka Controls Limited assemble a range of thermal switchgear.

The harbour is surprisingly busy with imports, mainly oil,

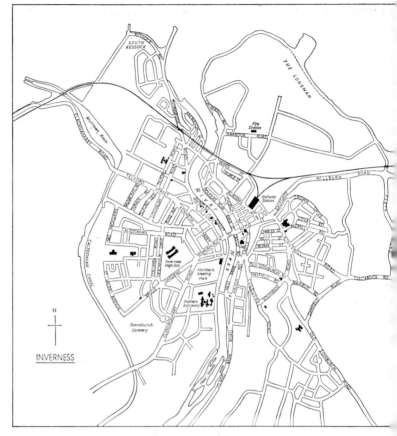

Street map of Inverness

timber, cement and steel worth £16,922,000 in 1972, while
exports, of which cured fish and grain were the main items, were
worth £7,198,000. Only three small fishing vessels still put to
sea from Inverness but the boats of the Lossiemouth fisheries
district all carry the registration letters INS. In winter the enclosed waters of the Beauly Firth become alive with shoals of
herring and sprats and some vessels land their catches at Inverness. Most of these fish find their way to the fish meal factory at

174

Fraserburgh but processing firms based at Inverness purchase considerable quantities for freezing.

Tourism is a major industry since Inverness is an ideal centre for touring the Moray Firth and some of Scotland's loveliest glens such as Glen Affric, Glen Cannich, Glen Moriston and Glen Shiel, while on its doorstep lies the famous Loch Ness. The town itself has many attractions—good hotels and restaurants, an art gallery and a museum that contains many relics of the area's fascinating history. Sporting facilities in Inverness include golf courses, tennis courts and bowling greens, and permits are available for anglers on the River Ness. There are many beauty spots along the river including the well-known Ness islands which lie less than a mile upstream from the town's centre. The islands are connected with each other and with the banks on either side by bridges; they are covered in trees and shrubs and are laid out with walks and flower beds. There is a bandstand where entertainment is provided each week-day from June to mid-September. On the west bank of the Ness is the Bught Park with a public recreation ground, sports pitches and a large municipal caravan site.

The most interesting building in Inverness is the castle, a fine Tudor building of red sandstone. Visitors are often disappointed to discover that the castle is so comparatively new, but to compensate is the knowledge that this spot has been dominated by a fortress for over 800 years, and in the courtyard is the well of the old castle rediscovered in 1909. The castle is used as administrative offices and as Sheriff Court House. On the castle esplanade stands a memorial to Flora MacDonald, the work of the Inverness sculptor Andrew Davidson, and erected in 1899.

Many people deplore the changes that have already taken place in Inverness; they regret the disappearance of the old suspension bridge that used to identify Inverness in any photograph and its replacement by one that has been called 'not so much a bridge as a road across the river'; there is criticism of the massive Bridge Street development of shops and offices that tend to dwarf the castle nearby. But Inverness is alive to its fine architectural heritage and many old buildings have been preserved or are in the process of being restored.

Recent developments have not altered the fundamental character of the riverside, and indeed it will be enhanced by the planned improvements which include the conversion of Eden Court next to the cathedral, once the Bishop's Palace. It is to become a cultural centre with conference hall and civic theatre. Lower down the river stands Balnain House, formerly the home of the Duffs of Drummuir, and the only early Georgian mansion still surviving in Inverness. It is to be restored as a visitors' centre with help from the Civic Trust.

Perhaps the most interesting street in Inverness is Church Street, with its blend of ancient and modern buildings, some dating back to the sixteenth century. It contains some of the town's finest architecture including the old High Church from which the street takes its name. The present building dates from 1770 but its tower and steeple are much older. Most outstanding is the restoration of Abertarff House which was built in 1593. Once belonging to Lord Lovat, chief of the clan Fraser, it has been since 1966 the headquarters of An Comunn Gaidhealach (The Highland Society). Now conspicuous with its white harled walls, picturesque crow-stepped gables and projecting stair tower, it is the only castellated mansion remaining in Inverness

Also in this street is the Dunbar Centre, built in 1688. It has been in turn an almshouse, hospital, library and school and has now returned to the service of elderly people as a recreational club. Next to the Dunbar Centre is Bow Court built in 1729 now housing on the ground floor an art salon and craft shop, while the two upper stories have been converted into exclusive three roomed flats. At the south end of the street at the junction with Bridge Street stands one of the best known landmarks of Inverness, the 155ft-high town steeple erected in 1791. The Prudential building which adjoins it was built in 1794 as the burgh courthouse.

176

Inverness will see many more changes in the next few years as the pace of industrialisation quickens in the whole Moray Firth area. The report of the Jack Holmes Planning Group, submitted to the Highlands and Islands Development Board in 1968, envisages a doubling of the population to 70,000 with a considerable expansion of service and manufacturing industries. It recognises the importance of Inverness as the gateway to the Moray Firth and realises the need for the various forms of transport to be properly integrated to make the town an efficient interchange.

Realignment of the A9 which will skirt the Longman industrial estate along its eastern side should remove a great part of the present traffic bottle-neck. In 1974 Inverness became the administrative centre for the new Highlands region making the town officially what it has been for so long—the capital of the Highlands.

L

10   THE PEOPLE

THE Highlands are poor in natural resources but rich in the character of their people. They are steeped in tradition and heritage and distinguished by a rare degree of individualism. Much of the character and temperament of the Highlander stems from his rugged environment which bred an independence and a dour determination to succeed in the face of apparently hopeless odds. These qualities were put to good use by many thousands of emigrants in the long era of Britain's colonial expansion but unfortunately the story of the Highlander in his own country is less bright.

The greatest tragedy was the decline of Gaelic language and culture in this area. It began with the breakdown of the clan system and accelerated in the aftermath of the '45 rebellion, being helped by the deliberate spread of the English educational system. The economic ills of the nineteenth century culminated in the clearances and the removal from the glens of whole communities of Gaelic-speaking people. Everything happened so quickly—the advent of the sheep farmers was almost as sudden as the abolition of the feudal system; the people were bewildered and it is no wonder that their culture suffered in the process, that the joy and happiness went from their poetry and music. But fortunately it did not vanish completely and there still survives in the Highlands a rich cultural tradition.

TRADITIONS

The origins of all aspects of Highland culture can be traced back through the centuries to the late Middle Ages when the

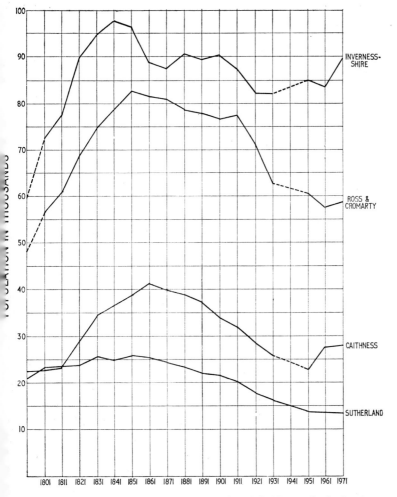

Population trends 1755–1971 for the counties of Caithness, Sutherland, Ross and Cromarty, and Inverness-shire

chiefs were still patriarchal figures and not the feudal landlords
into which they degenerated. In their great castles they surrounded themselves with poets and musicians and entertained
their guests with banquets at which the bard related the heroic
deeds of the clan's heroes and extolled the virtues of the chief's
ancestors. Two important men in the chief's household were his
harper who played the ancient musical instrument, the clarsach,
and the piper who played the bagpipes. The ordinary people,
too, whiled away the long winter evenings with music and
dance and with listening to tales of early Celtic heroes.

Music and dance were the two essential accompaniments to
Gaelic ritual—at weddings, christenings and harvest festivals
the people danced in the open air to the skirl of the pipes and
indoors to the scrape of the fiddle. After a funeral, too, the
people joined in a dance but there was no callousness in this
rite, the dance added dignity to a solemn occasion. If the
funeral was in honour of a man of importance the mourners
wailed a coronach—a song praising the qualities of the deceased.
In everyday life singing accompanied the reaping of the grain
and the fulling of the cloth and it timed the rhythmic beat of the
boatman's oars.

Although it was a life of poverty punctuated by tragedy one
thing was constant—the companionship of the clans. The sense
of oneness and belonging to a greater unit was fostered by
fanatical loyalty to the chief and in the seventeenth century or
even earlier, by the wearing of plant badges and the use of a
clan motto. Some of the plant symbols may have been adopted
in the nature of a talisman, a protection from illness or witchcraft but some may have been adopted spontaneously. The
MacDonalds wore a sprig of heather, the MacDougalls chose
bell heather while juniper was the symbol of the clans Gunn,
MacLeod and Ross. The adoption of a specific tartan may be of
quite recent origin but as long ago as the sixteenth century
women knew how to weave woollen cloth in a checked pattern
from wool coloured with natural dyes.

There have been many arguments about the supposed evolution of Highland dress. It is believed that the saffron yellow tunic originating in Ireland was worn in the Highlands until the end of the sixteenth century when it was replaced by the great belted plaid—the forerunner of Highland dress as we know it. The belted plaid was a length of tartan about 18ft long and 5ft wide, wrapped around the waist and crossed in front to hang in low folds reaching to the knees. It was held secure by a leather belt around the waist. The surplus material was used as a cloak, one end fastened at the left shoulder with a brooch, while the other longer end was tucked inside the belt at the back. The belted plaid or *filleadh mor* was a cumbersome piece of apparel and early in the eighteenth century it gave way to the philibeg (Anglicised spelling) or small kilt which is the essential feature of Highland dress today.

After Culloden the Act for the Abolition and Proscription of the Highland Dress made it illegal for any civilian to wear the plaid or philibeg 'or any part whatsoever of what peculiarly belongs to the Highland garb', with the result that when the act was finally repealed in 1782 the women of the clans had lost the skill of weaving tartan. Other traditions suffered too and in 1821 Colonel David Stewart could write 'much of the romance and chivalry of the Highland character is gone. The voice of the bard has long been silent and poetry, tradition and song are vanishing away'. The clarsach was practically extinct, the bagpipes rare and the great piping schools of the MacCrimmons and the MacArthurs merely a memory.

One reason for the survival of Highland traditions was that Scottish regiments were allowed to wear Highland dress, the government not daring to let this aspect of the Highland fighting tradition die. So the skirl of the pipes were heard at the relief of Lucknow and on the Heights of Abraham, while in peacetime crowds thrilled to the sight of pipe bands marching and counter-marching, moving in complicated patterns, the bandsmen resplendent in feathered bonnet, tartan kilt, plaid and hose. The tunes themselves bore witness to the valour of the Highland soldier from 'The Barren Rocks of Aden' to 'The Green Hills of Tyrol'.

Scotland awoke to a new awareness of the tradition she had almost lost. King George IV visited Edinburgh in 1822, a brave figure in full Highland dress, and the growing interest developed into a vogue. A rush began to find out to which clan one was affiliated and which tartan one was entitled to wear, and for those who could not find a clan or tartan there were entrepreneurs willing to invent both. It is significant that most of the tartans of today cannot be traced back further than the early nineteenth century.

The revival extended to an interest in everything Highland which Lowland manufacturers and shopkeepers turned to their advantage with a flood of cheap tartan souvenirs, tartan dresses and even tartan curtains in the drawing-room. But while Highland culture seemed to be in full bloom its roots were slowly being destroyed, for ironically this revival coincided with the clearances, the real clansmen being hounded like vermin from their poor homes.

In 1891 An Comunn Gaidhealach was formed determined to separate the genuine Gaelic culture from the false face of commercialism. It came just in time, for in 1891 only two clarsachs were known to survive. Lord Archibald Campbell, the society's first president, started a revival when he ordered nine new instruments to be made, and today there are more players than at any time since the Middle Ages with the regular appearance of the clarsach at Gaelic festivals and concerts, and on TV.

All the glory of Highland tradition is concentrated in the Highland gatherings that take place in towns and villages each summer. Athletes compete in ancient sports like running, wrestling and tossing the caber, the kilts swing in dancing competitions and the music of the bagpipes floods the games park. Such gatherings are held far beyond the confines of the Highlands, even in territories overseas where Highlanders have settled in sufficient numbers. Lowland Scottish regiments too have adopted Highland traditions and one of the finest displays of Scottish military pageantry is seen at the military tattoo held each year at Edinburgh Castle. During the Edinburgh Festival one of the sights most appreciated by visitors is the march along Prince's Street of the Edinburgh City Police Pipe Band.

The kilt and the bagpipes are now symbols of Scotland, not just of the Highlands alone. The hitch-hiker who wears a kilt during his holiday on the continent has a better chance of getting a lift and the Scottish businessman on a business trip to America has a better chance of securing orders if he wears the kilt. So in a way Gaeldom has triumphed over its enemies and especially over those who tried to kill it more than 200 years ago.

FOLKLORE

There is a long tradition of story-telling in the Highlands for in the absence of books the bard took the place of the library and many of his stories have survived from prehistoric times. James MacPherson (1736–1796) recorded fragments of ancient poetry and translated them from the Gaelic, claiming that they were tales told by the third-century bard, Ossian. These poems and later works were enthusiastically received but they sparked off a tremendous literary controversy, one of MacPherson's most formidable opponents being Dr Johnson who questioned their authenticity. MacPherson countered by publishing the Gaelic 'text' of his translations but the controversy continued. Subsequent enquiry shows that although these poems are based to some extent on oral traditions they are in no sense genuine translations. But their strange romantic ideas, and the wild grandeur of their scenic background caught contemporary imagination. Ossian was translated into all the main European languages and was a powerful influence in the Romantic revival.

It was a fact accepted by early Highlanders that the earth was inhabited with other creatures besides men and animals.

There were giants and dwarfs who resembled men, but there were others such as kelpies who lived in lochs and rivers and sometimes appeared in the shape of a man or a horse. Many of the region's topographical features were explained by reference to the actions of these creatures; for example the Sutors of Cromarty were supposed to have been giants who broke some primeval law and were turned into these headlands where they still stand guarding the entrance to the Cromarty Firth.

The introduction of Christianity gave rise to a rich crop of legends in the Highlands—stories that can have no basis in history. It has long been known that the sweetest tasting fish in the North Sea are the small herring caught at Kessock. An old legend declares that this is the same species that swims in the Sea of Galilee and that when St Joseph of Arimathea carried the Stone of Destiny to Scotland his food supplies consisted mainly of these little herring dried and cured. After his long journey he had grown rather tired of his monotonous diet and threw the remaining fish into the sea. God restored life to them and they swam searching in vain for an inland sea such as the one they had left, and finally chose the quiet waters of the Beauly Firth as the best substitute.

The early Celtic saints are remembered by a hopeless confusion of historical fact and legend handed down by word of mouth and embellished in the process. When St Columba approached King Bridei's fort beside the River Ness the great gates were shut against him but he traced the sign of the cross and the gates flew open of their own accord. Sometimes the priests enlisted the help of the mysterious creatures of the hills to help them. The water horses were especially co-operative because they loved theological discussions and were concerned about their souls although uncertain whether they possessed such things. The kelpie of Loch Shin offered to help the local priest to build a church if he might thereby gain a soul. He knew of a ruined dun nearby and carried the stones across the

184

loch to the new site, but the dun was a fairy dwelling and the kelpie was unpopular in supernatural circles thereafter. The priest having got his church built is believed to have made little effort in obtaining a soul for the kelpie.

The Norsemen came with their stories of Odin, Thor and Freyja and the people of the north began to see what appeared to be men on the lonely moors but were really gods in disguise. Their disguise was imperfect for they wore cloaks of blue—the colour of the night sky—a shade that no human dyer could achieve.

With the teaching of Christianity there came a polarisation of good and evil, the latter being personified in Satan and his servants such as witches, wizards and demons. There were people too who had the power of calling upon Satan to help them, one of these being Michael Scott, the famous wizard. He raised the devil in the form of three small demons who worked for him, and performed many tasks for his friends but he discovered that he did not have sufficient work to satisfy them. He began to travel and wherever he stopped for the night he ordered them to build a palace and then demolish it in the morning. On his strange journey he arrived at Inverness and in three nights' work his demons succeeded in building a wooden bridge over the River Ness.

Another feat attempted by Michael Scott's demons was the building of a causeway between Fortrose and Ardersier. They would have succeeded too had not a shepherd seen the strange little fellows at work and, alarmed, called out for the blessing of God on their work. The devils fled but their unfinished work stands today.

Michael Scott tried to elude his companions by riding non-stop from Caithness to the Cromarty Firth and then leaping from the North to the South Sutor (the marks of his horse's hooves used to be seen at both places); but before he had regained his breath he heard the hated voices at his side: 'work, master, more work.'

The wizard eventually found a job to keep them occupied—one not yet completed. He ordered them to make a rope of sand long enough to girdle the earth and bind the moon to the earth. One can still see these ropes at low tide on sandy beaches but always the tide returns and washes them away.

Even in comparatively recent times the peoples' lives were dominated by supernatural beings. Any unusual place such as the Hill of Tom-na-Hurich near Inverness or the Dell of Eathie in the Black Isle was bound to be the haunt of fairies. At the latter place people at times heard the sound of bagpipes played by a piper imprisoned by the fairies deep inside the red sandstone cliffs. Water horses continued to terrorise travellers on lonely moors and the rougher the terrain the more fearsome was the creature who lived there. On the bleak moors of Sutherland, up near Cape Wrath, lived the Cu-Saeng, a terrible monster whom to meet was death.

There was no clear dividing line between the natural and supernatural for animals might be spirits or demons in disguise and old people when they died were supposed to return as seagulls or as seals. Seals have many stories associated with them. Sometimes they were supposed to take human forms after casting off their skins and concealing them in a cave; they were then very vulnerable, however, as if their skins were stolen they were unable to return to the sea with their companions. From Loch Duich comes the tale of three brothers who married three seal maidens after hiding their skins.

Considering the long history of violence and death it is not surprising that ghosts figure prominently in Highland folklore and there is an eerie story associated with almost every ruined church and castle. Some people were credited with the ability to predict the death of their friends and even today the gift of 'second-sight' is attributed to many people.

Best known of all Highland soothsayers is Kenneth Odhar MacKenzie who, although born about 1600 in Lewis, spent most of his life as a common labourer on the estate of Brahan, hence the title by which he is best known—the Brahan seer. There are several different versions of how he acquired the blue stone with the hole in the middle which, when he peered through it, allowed him to foretell future events.

One day a gentleman from Inverness visited the seer and asked him to return to Inverness where a clerk would record his predictions. A number of predictions were recorded then the seer continued: 'The time will come, and it is not far off, when a full-rigged ship will be seen sailing eastward and westward by the back of Tom-na-Hurich.' At this time the gentleman told the clerk to shut his book for this nonsense was not worth recording. The gentleman did not live to see the prediction fulfilled but in 1822 the Caledonian Canal was opened and ships began sailing past Tom-na-Hurich.

His ability to foresee the future was the cause of his own death. The Earl of Seaforth was on a visit to Paris and Lady Seaforth, after some months, became anxious for his safety. She summoned Kenneth Odhar and asked him to find out if her husband was safe. On putting the stone to his eye Kenneth replied that he was not only safe but merry and happy. Lady Seaforth insisted on having more details and the seer reluctantly described the scene at Paris—how her husband was kneeling beside a fair lady, her hand pressed to his lips. All the jealousy and humiliation of the Countess was turned on poor Kenneth and she ordered that he should be put to death.

Before his death in a barrel of blazing tar Kenneth Odhar made his most famous prophecy—he foretold the doom of the house of Seaforth. The last chief would be deaf and dumb, he would have four sons who would all die before him and a 'white-coifed lassie from the East' would succeed him and kill her sister. As a warning sign to the last earl there would be four great chiefs in the Highlands, one buck-toothed, one hare-lipped, one half-witted and the fourth a stammerer. It all came true and the daughter who succeeded Lord Seaforth in 1815 was a widow (white-coifed) who had spent some time in India.

One day while driving on the estate the horses bolted and killed her sister.

The prophecies of the Brahan seer have received much attention in the Highlands and steps have been taken at times to prevent the required conditions being achieved. Earlier this century when St Anne's Episcopal Church was being built at Strathpeffer, local people insisted that it should have no steeple because the seer had prophesied that when five spires rose in Strathpeffer ships would sail over the village and anchor to a spire. Protests were of no avail and the people counted their five steeples and waited for something to happen. This came in 1920 when a small airship flew in for the Strathpeffer games and in descending dropped a grapnel which caught on one of the spires.

Some of Kenneth Odhar's prophecies read almost like a history of the Highlands .'The day will come when the jaw-bone of the big sheep will put the plough on the rafters; when sheep shall become so numerous that the bleating of the one shall be heard by the other from Conchra in Lochalsh to Bun-da-Loch in Kintail . . . The ancient proprietors of the soil shall give place to strange merchant proprietors, and the whole Highlands will become one huge deer forest; the whole country will be so utterly desolated and depopulated that the crow of a cock shall not be heard north of Druim-Uachdair; the people will emigrate to islands now unknown, but which shall yet be discovered in the boundless oceans.' The final part of this prophecy is that the deer and other wild animals will be exterminated by 'horrid black rain', after which the people will return and take undisturbed possession of the lands of their ancestors. There are some who today see in this a reference to North Sea oil.

RELIGION

To understand the complexity of religious beliefs in the Highlands it is necessary to go back again to the days before the

Reformation. The need for changes was obvious since the great abbeys and priories had fallen into the hands of favourites and even illegitimate sons of the royal house and high offices were occupied by men who cared little for the souls of their people but merely wished to enjoy the revenues their position brought them.

But it was not merely a change the Scottish reformers wanted —they wanted a new faith. The main point in their teachings was reliance upon scriptural proof for the ordinances of the church—a church free from all man-made ceremony. In the Roman Church the scriptures were regarded as a holy mystery to be interpreted by the priest to the people, but in 1530 copies of Tyndale's translation of the New Testament were circulating in Scotland and the reformers could use it to justify their claims.

The name of John Knox stands out among the Scottish reformers. He was influenced by John Calvin who stressed the importance of private prayer and Bible reading and the simplicity of church ritual, and it was Knox who promoted the reformation of 1560 although Andrew Melville was the man who promoted presbyterianism, a system of church government based on government by the people. In the Scottish system each church is governed by a kirk session consisting of the minister and church elders, and a hierarchy of presbyteries and synods leads up to the General Assembly which meets in Edinburgh each year.

In 1592 the Scottish Church became Presbyterian by law but King James VI succeeded in restoring government by bishops in 1610 and the next eighty years saw a continuing struggle between the two forms until finally in 1690, after the crowning of William and Mary, it was decreed that the church should be Presbyterian since this was 'agreeable to the inclination of the generality of the people'.

The Church made little headway at first in the Highlands in spite of an act passed in 1700 for preventing the 'growth of popery', but in 1724 several presbyteries were set up forming the synod of Glenelg and in 1726 the presbytery of Tongue was established. After 1745 the Episcopal Church was in disgrace for its alleged support of the Stuarts, its meeting houses were closed and a clergyman of that church who held services or prayed with more than four persons was liable to imprisonment for a first offence and for a subsequent conviction, transportation for life. The Church of Scotland took advantage of this spiritual vacuum to extend its own power, aided considerably by teachers and catechists of the Society (in Scotland) for Propagating Christian Knowledge which had been set up in 1709.

The Church of Scotland was soon to be plagued by controversy for in 1712 the right to appoint ministers was removed from the congregation and given to the landlords. The Patronage Act caused a series of splits in the mid-eighteenth century which worsened gradually until 1843 when the split between the two main factions was so great that an act commonly referred to as the Disruption took place. The upshot of this was that 500 ministers and almost half its members seceded from the Church of Scotland to form their own Free Church of Scotland. This was a rival organisation complete with kirk sessions, presbyteries and synods and its own General Assembly, and resulted in the building of rival churches and manses often next to those of the 'Auld Kirk'.

The question of patronage was not the only factor in the Disruption. The Church of Scotland had been accused of remaining silent to the great social problems of the age, the chief of which was the clearances, but those who seceded also felt that the church had slipped away from its strict Calvinist principles and they were determined to re-establish the puritanism of the seventeenth century.

Feelings ran high in the Highlands and in places bitter hatred ensued. Almost the entire congregation at Strontian seceded from the Church of Scotland but the landlord refused to give them a site for their church. They held services in the open air for a time, then they had a 'floating church' built in a Clyde shipyard and in 1846 it was towed to an anchorage out of sight of the uncooperative landlord. It blew ashore a few years later but the congregation continued to assemble in it until a site for a proper church was acquired in 1873.

The offending Patronage Act was removed in 1874 thus paving the way for partial reunion of the churches, but not before further splits occurred. In 1900 the Free Church broke into two, most of its members and ministers joining with the United Presbyterian Church to form the United Free Church, while the minority chose to remain loyal to the Free Church. In 1929 the United Free Church and the Church of Scotland reunited, but the Free Church still retains its separate identity. It is a strict denomination, evangelical in its teaching, and frowning on worldly pursuits such as cinema-going and dancing, and insisting on complete observance of the Sabbath day. It has from time to time found it necessary to criticise the Duke of Edinburgh for playing polo on Sunday.

The Church of Scotland is by far the strongest denomination in the Highlands but the Roman Catholic Church is well represented in a belt between Inverness and the island of Barra, while the Episcopal Church continues to claim its descent from the early Scottish reformation church. There are Congregational and Baptist churches, both of them derived from religious revivals of the late eighteenth century, while numerous small denominations are represented covering the complete spectrum of religion. Church-going and Sabbath observance are as much a part of the Highlands as is their Gaelic heritage, although all three are currently declining through external influences.

EDUCATION

There was a grammar school at Inverness soon after the Reformation but more than a hundred years elapsed before the rest of the area received attention. In 1696 an Act of Parliament made it compulsory for landowners to establish a school in every parish, but it was less successful in the Highlands than in the Lowlands since Highland parishes were so large that only the part nearest the school benefited.

The founding of the SSPCK in 1709 was of tremendous importance in the Highlands and by 1758 it had provided 176 schools. In 1811 the Gaelic Society of Edinburgh began to give special attention to Gaelic-speaking areas where an education in English was far from satisfactory. This was followed by the Gaelic Society of Glasgow in 1812 and the Gaelic Society of Inverness in 1818. In 1825 a survey made by the Gaelic Society of Inverness and covering 500 schools and 25,000 pupils revealed that only one-third of them were provided under the statutory parochial system, the rest being provided by the SSPCK and the three Gaelic societies. The teaching success varied—in Wester Ross and west Inverness-shire only three children in ten could read while in Easter Ross, east Inverness-shire, Sutherland and Caithness, the proportion was six in ten.

The buildings were bleak and cheerless, school meals unheard of; candles were required to give a little light in winter and each child had to bring a peat to school as his contribution to the heating system. But the teachers did a remarkable job and many a Highland child received the basic ground-work that prepared him for one of Scotland's four universities; while along the coast, especially in Caithness, several schools were noted for their teaching of navigation.

The Education Act of 1872 transferred the running of all these schools to newly elected Parish School Boards whose aim was to provide elementary education (now compulsory) to all children between the ages of five and thirteen, and to provide additional schools where necessary.

One of the most obvious changes since 1872 is the reduction in the number of schools; for example in the early 1920s Caithness had 68 schools but 50 years later only 28. Rural depopulation is one of the reasons for this but the Education Act of 1946 which made attendance at a secondary school compulsory from the age of twelve, had the effect of removing more pupils from small schools and making some of them no longer viable. Nowadays the educationalists' belief that children benefit by being taught in fairly large numbers has led to the closure of still more schools.

The standard of education in the Highlands is among the best in Britain, modern school buildings and small classes being a feature of the entire area. Many of the schools have emerged with credit from national competitions and in 1970 a team from Inverness Royal Academy were finalists in TV's Top of the Form. Inverness Technical College has been expanded considerably and now has a roll of over 3,000 students drawn from all over the Highlands and islands. Its range of studies covers the entire range of Highland industries.

GAELIC LANGUAGE

At the time of its maximum extension Gaelic was spoken over practically the whole of Scotland but a steady contraction set in under the relentless advance of English and the Lowland dialect 'Scots'. There arose the distinction in people's minds between the 'civilised' English-speaking Lowlands and the wild Gaelic-speaking Highlands. There was even a theory that if it were possible to eradicate the Gaelic language the Highlanders would become 'civilised', so the Statutes of Iona enacted in 1609 decreed that wealthy Highland gentlemen should send their eldest child to be educated in the Lowlands. It is significant that in the seventeenth century Gaelic poets complained that the chiefs were no longer patrons of the arts.

After 1745 the campaign against Gaelic intensified in the lunatic belief that the language was in some way responsible for the rebellion. Gaelic could not be banned like Highland dress but the campaign against it was as effective—Jacobite chiefs were removed from contact with their people and when they returned they were in all respects English. More insidious was the campaign of well meaning churchmen who zealously set out to light the Highlands with the twin torches of Calvinism and the English language. They relented when they realised the strength of Gaelic and by 1767 the New Testament was available in a Gaelic translation.

The language continued to flourish in the north, and in Sutherland the poet Rob Donn MacKay (1714–1778) left a rich store of poems which were preserved orally until 1829 when they were committed to paper. But the happiness of the Gael was soon to be destroyed as the clearances emptied the glens and the Black Face sheep began to shelter in the ruins of mountain shielings.

Even in the eighteenth century there were those who championed Gaelic, in particular the societies of Edinburgh, Glasgow and Inverness which encouraged Highlanders to become literate in their own language. Gaelic periodicals began to appear in which the Highlander could read articles on international and domestic affairs. Then in 1872 the Education Act, however well intended, imposed on the Highlands the English system of education and actually opposed the use of Gaelic as a medium of instruction.

This was the biggest blow of all to Gaelic language and culture. It was a terrible experience for a child of five or six to start school and then discover his form of speech was considered inferior. The people gave in and crofters believed that the best legacy they could ensure for their children was a good education, fluency in English and the prospect of a good job beyond the mountains or across the sea. Those who remained became bilingual and many tried to hinder their children from picking up Gaelic to spare them the humiliating discovery at school that their native language was considered uncultured.

The Gaelic language would have vanished entirely from the mainland had it not been for the efforts of educated Highlanders such as those who grouped together in 1871 to form the

Inverness Gaelic Society to campaign for better treatment. In 1891 An Comunn Gaidhealach was formed to promote the language, its literature and other traditions. It is a voluntary organisation and is still extremely active today but without official recognition of Gaelic and the treatment usually given to minority languages, much of the society's efforts are cancelled out. The fact is that since 1872 the number of Gaelic-speakers in Scotland has declined by 150,000 and today there are fewer than 80,000 of them, most of them in the Hebrides.

A concession was made in the Education Act of 1918 for the teaching of Gaelic but until comparatively recently it was regarded as a special subject to be taught through the English language. Lately a more enlightened attitude emerged especially in the former counties of Ross and Cromarty and Inverness-shire, whose education committees were the first to reintroduce Gaelic as a teaching medium in areas where it is still the local tongue. In Inverness there is even a Gaelic play-group for children of pre-school age.

There is still a rich living culture which is seen best at the annual National Mod, which is for Gaeldom what the Eisteddfod is for Wales. It is not always held in the Highlands for in 1973 it was held at Ayr where there are now very few native Gaelic speakers, but a glance at the place-names on the map show that at one time Gaelic held sway here too. As well as competitors from the strongholds of Gaeldom in Lewis, Harris, the Uists and Skye, people came from all over Scotland and even from Nova Scotia where they learn Gaelic with a Canadian accent. There are competitions for choirs, vocalists, intrumentalists, fiddle groups, pipers and Gaelic folk groups all hoping to carry off a coveted gold medal.

Gaelic is an ancient language; it was spoken by the Scots who came from Ireland in the fifth century AD; it was the language of the Celtic monks who brought Christianity and culture to Britain and much of Europe; it is the oldest institution in Scotland and it must not be allowed to die.

The contribution by Highlanders in Britain's colonial expansion and in Britain's wars in every corner of the globe is out of all proportion to the total size and population of their homeland. As early as 1626 MacKay's Regiment was raised by Sir Donald MacKay of Strathnaver and fought on the continent for the Protestant kings in the Thirty Years War. The Highlanders played a decisive part in the revolution of 1688 for when William of Orange arrived in Britain he already had his own Highland troops commanded by General Hugh MacKay, a native of Scourie. How tragic it was that in the campaign that followed Protestant Highlander was fighting against Catholic Highlander—a phenomenon that was often to be repeated during the next half-century.

MacKay's Regiment was the precursor of many more Highland regiments. In 1739 companies of Highlanders loyal to the government were raised for police duties and they became the nucleus of one of the most famous regiments of all—The Black Watch. Between 1757 and 1766 eleven more regiments were raised including the Fraser Highlanders who achieved distinction fighting under General Wolfe at Quebec.

The Highland regiments played a great part in the two world wars of the twentieth century—30,000 men served in the Black Watch in World War I, 8,000 of them being killed at such battles as Arras, Ypres and Passchendaele. But it is unfair to single out one regiment, as equally worthy of mention were the Seaforth Highlanders, the Queen's Own Cameron Highlanders, the Argyll and Sutherland Highlanders and the Lovat Scouts.

One of the most famous Highland soldiers of all time was Sir Hector MacDonald or 'Fighting Mac' as he was affectionately known. Born in the Black Isle, he commanded the Highland Brigade in the Boer War but he died tragically in Paris in 1903. He is commemorated by a statue at Dingwall. The present chief of the clan Fraser, Lord Lovat, achieved fame as a commando leader in World War II.

The Highlands have produced famous explorers too. One of them, Simon Fraser, helped to open up the Canadian west and discovered and gave his name to the Fraser River in British Columbia. Alexander MacKenzie who gave his name to the MacKenzie River which he followed to its outlet in the Arctic Ocean, returned to Scotland about 1800 and is buried in Avoch cemetery.

Caithness has produced a surprising number of eminent men including Sir John Sinclair who did so much to improve agriculture by abolishing the open field system and introducing regular crop rotation. He was responsible for compiling the first 'statistical account of Scotland' in 1790—indeed it was he who coined the word 'statistics'. A leader in a different field was Sir William Smith, founder of the Boys' Brigade who was born at Thurso in 1854.

Reference has been made earlier to Hugh Miller. Born at Cromarty in 1802 he became a stonemason at the age of seventeen but through working with the sandstone rocks of the Black Isle he became interested in geology and made a special study of the group of sedimentary rocks known as Old Red Sandstone. He became interested in writing as a hobby and his first published work was an article in the *Inverness Courier* on the herring fishery. A book of poems followed in 1829, and in 1835 a book entitled *Scenes and Legends of the North of Scotland*. He was possessed of strong religious views and in 1840 was invited to Edinburgh to become editor of the evangelical newspaper, *The Witness*. His best known scientific work *The Old Red Sandstone* appeared in 1841 and in 1852 his autobiography *My Schools and Schoolmasters*.

The publication of *The Old Red Sandstone* acted as a spur to another amateur, Robert Dick, baker in Thurso, who became an authority on both botany and geology. It was he who rediscovered Northern holygrass, a plant which had been thought extinct. He was a modest man and never wrote for publication, but he corresponded with Hugh Miller who subsequently made considerable modifications to the text of *The Old Red Sandstone*. He later wrote to Dick: 'He has robbed himself to do me service.' Robert Dick's business ended in ruin and he spent the last two years of his life in great privation. He died in 1866 and the townspeople gave him a public funeral in recognition of a great man. The Dick collection of plants, fossils and shells on display in Thurso museum is a remarkable testimony to the enthusiasm of this self-taught amateur.

The best known Highlander of this century was the novelist Neil M. Gunn who was born at Dunbeath, Caithness in 1891. The son of a fisherman, he had a typical Highland upbringing, his parents being keen that he receive a good education to enable him to find a good job. He entered the civil service, joining the Customs & Excise which was the only service to offer posts in the Highlands.

His writing career began with short stories published in 1920 and after settling in Inverness his first novel, *The Grey Coast*, was published in 1926. Others followed including *Morning Tide* in 1931, *The Lost Glen* in 1932, *Butcher's Broom* in 1934, *Wild Geese Overhead* in 1939. Writing brought financial independence and he gave up his job in the civil service to set up house with his wife in the hills near Strathpeffer. Here he wrote his major work *The Silver Darlings* which depicts the toil, hardship, heartbreak and heroism of the herring fishermen on the Moray Firth in the nineteenth century.

His last book, an autobiography entitled *The Atom of Delight*, was published in 1956. Unfortunately this was one of his least successful works, but already his reputation was assured as the greatest Scottish novelist since Sir Walter Scott. He died in January 1973.

LIVING CONDITIONS TODAY

There have been many changes in the last few decades: the old 'black' house with its thatched roof and earthen floor has disappeared being replaced with two-storey slate-roofed croft houses or modern bungalows; the well stocked deep-freeze has taken the place of the store of dried fish and barrel of salt herring; water is now piped from a public supply and electric light has banished the Tilley lamp to a shelf in the attic. The people have shared in all the benefits of the welfare state and the advent of TV has reduced the feeling of remoteness.

But some things do not change: crofting is still an uncertain business—wet summers still mean difficulties in drying the hay, life without a part-time job and a weekly wage is as difficult as ever. But there are prospects of more jobs and these are welcome so long as they do not swamp the Highland way of life.

There is so much in the old way of life that is worth saving: the self-sufficiency and quiet commonsense of the natural life; the co-operation that is so essential to living in remote places, still seen in the communal operation of herding the sheep for dipping or clipping; the unselfishness of caring for elderly neighbours. There are lessons here for all of us.

11   PLACES TO VISIT

FOR 200 years the northern Highlands have attracted
tourists from other parts of Britain and from overseas.
Visitors may admire the splendid peaks of Canisp and
Suilven, marvel at the waterfalls of Eas Coul Aulin or Corrieshalloch Gorge, gaze in awe at the high sea-cliffs of Cape Wrath
or Duncansby Head, but views alone can tell them little of the
underlying story of the region, of how rocks, soil, climate and
the effects of man have produced what we see today. It is a
fascinating story but it needs the specialist knowledge of the
geographer, naturalist, archaeologist and historian to make it
come alive. Fortunately such information is becoming more
readily available to the enquiring visitor with pamphlets from
such organisations as An Comunn Gaidhealach and the
Countryside Commission for Scotland as they begin to tap this
wealth of material.

PREHISTORIC SITES

The oldest man-made structures in the Highlands are the
strange burial mounds from Neolithic or New Stone Age times
5,000 years ago. There are several types but most are built on
the same principle—a walled passage leads to a central chamber, often subdivided, where interment took place and the
whole structure was effectively placed underground by covering
it with a huge mound of stones, leaving the entrance clear but
covered by a stone slab.

Such cairns are particularly common in Caithness where two

types occur—long cairns and round cairns. Enormous quantities of material were used in their construction—the 'long' cairn of Camster is 200ft by 65ft and contains an estimated 3,000 tons of stones. The 'round' cairns comprise a roughly oval chamber divided into three sections; the roof of the outer chamber is continuous with that of the low passage but the inner two compartments have corbelled roofs, each course of masonry overlapping on the one below. The best example of this type—the 'round' cairn at Camster—is probably the finest chambered tomb on the mainland of Britain.

In Sutherland there is a chambered tomb at Evelix in a field on the south side of the A9 and at Clashmore north of the A9. At Embo just outside the gate of the caravan site at Grannie's Hielan Hame there are two burial chambers, while another has been found at Old Hill, Lairg.

As the Bronze Age replaced the Stone Age in the northern Highlands, the building of cairns gradually ceased and the most common of Bronze Age remains are the mysterious standing stones again best represented in Caithness. The best example is the group of some 200 stones arranged in 22 parallel rows at Mid Clyth. The signpost beside the A9 reads appropriately 'Hill of Many Stones'. A group of 13 rows occurs at Upper Dounreay, 6 rows stand at Garrywhin and there are traces of 20 rows of small stones at Dirlot. Ruined stone circles are found at Guidebest and Broubster, pairs of standing stones at Loch of Yarrows and Latheron and single monoliths stand at Reay, Watten and the Hill of Rangag. The whole area between Camster and Loch of Yarrows is packed with archaeological treasures.

Probably the best known of prehistoric buildings are the brochs now reduced to heaps of rubble but which were originally defensive towers up to 60ft high guarding strategic headlands, glens and mountain passes. They are most numerous in Caithness and Sutherland but one or two are found in Ross and Cromarty and a pair of well preserved brochs stand at Glenelg on the Sound of Sleat. One of the best examples is Dun Dorna-dilla which stands in Strathmore south of Loch Hope in Suther-land, another is at Carn Liath near Dunrobin, its entrance facing south-east towards the Moray Firth.

A good example of the vitrified fort is the dun of Creich on a hill-top south of the main A9, three miles east of Bonar Bridge. The ruins of Urquhart Castle stand in their turn on the ruins of a vitrified fort.

Many Pictish symbol stones have been found in this area, the best of them now removed to the safety of museums. The earliest stones had designs incised upon them by a chisel or sharp point and of these the stone found at Golspie is considered the most remarkable for the sensitivity of its lines. It is now in Dunrobin museum. Another Pictish sculptured stone is the Eagle stone near Strathpeffer, and two stones from the early Christian period can be seen in the parish of Nigg. One of them stands under the porch of the old parish church while the other stands in a field overlooking the village of Shandwick.

Most elaborate of all, representing the peak of Pictish art is the sculptured stone found at Hilton of Cadboll in Easter Ross. It has two panels the lower of which depicts a hunting scene with two huntsmen and their dogs, a trumpeter, and a figure believed to represent some Pictish chieftainess riding side-saddle on her horse. The upper panel features the common Pictish symbol, a broken rod superimposed upon a crescent and both panels are surrounded by elaborate scroll work. Standing almost 8ft high, it has been called 'more like the page of a manuscript than a stone'. It can be seen in the National Museum of Antiquities in Edinburgh.

CASTLES

After a long tradition of building in stone, culminating in the era of the brochs, there was a break until the medieval period of castle building. The earliest of these castles date from the twelfth century when Scotland was being feudalised and Anglo-Norman knights were seeking to consolidate their power in the Highlands by building fortresses. The earliest castles, however, were not of stone; they consisted of a high round mound of earth—the motte—crowned by a wooden tower, the whole being surrounded by a fosse and timber palisade. Some of these structures still survive as grass-covered mounds usually commanding strategic positions as at Holm south of Inverness and at Torvean, these two controlling the old ford over the River Ness. The original castle at Urquhart was of motte and bailey type and the ruins of Dunscaith castle founded by William the Lion opposite the town of Cromarty suggest that it too was a motte castle.

By the mid-thirteenth century a new era in stone building was in full swing with the two elements of the motte castle continuing. The tower became the thick-walled keep, the timber palisade developed into a high 'curtain' wall. An interesting early type of castle is known appropriately as the west Highland castle. Irregular in plan and of four, five or six sides, it usually dominated a rocky islet or promontory utilising the sheer cliffs below as part of the defence. The landward connection was protected by a ditch. The essential element of the west Highland castle was a high enclosing wall inside which the dwellings were built in the nature of lean-tos. There was only one door and few windows and along the top ran a parapet crenellated in places.

Mingary Castle, standing on a magnificent site commanding both Loch Sunart and the Sound of Mull, is a good example of this type. Its massive curtain wall 200ft in circumference, 25ft high and 6ft wide dates from the thirteenth century. This was the stronghold of the MacIans of Ardnamurchan, a sept of the Clan Donald and it played a major role in Scottish history. James IV chose this as his headquarters in his campaign to subdue the islesmen in 1493 and 1495; it was besieged several times by the MacLeans; in 1644 it was captured by Montrose's troops and used as a prison for some of the early supporters of the Covenant. Castle Tioram is another good example of this type and the original castle at Eilean Donan was also a typical west Highland castle.

From this type of castle there developed the curtain wall castle with towers at one or more of its corners, the thirteenth-century castle of Inverlochy being a good example. Yet another type had a curtain wall and a massive frontal gate house. One of the most interesting of all Scotland's ruined castles is Urquhart Castle that stands beside Loch Ness. Its great walls, its passages, arches and stairs and the massive tower at the north-east corner still suggest how impressive it must have been when built in the reign of Edward I. It was blown up in 1692 to prevent it falling into the hands of the Jacobites.

At the other end of the Highlands, in Caithness where Norse influence was strong, a different type of castle developed—a simple fortified tower built close to the cliffs. Braal Castle was built in the thirteenth century and is associated with Harold, Earl of Caithness, and the castle of Old Wick may well have been built by the Norsemen. It stands on a promontory cut off from the land by a ditch and defended on its other sides by sheer cliffs.

Most of Scotland's castles date from the great period of building in the fifteenth and sixteenth centuries. The basis was the fortified tower house but later types have one or two projecting wings giving rise to L, Z or E types of castle. There are dozens of them in the Highlands, some of them occupying spectacular positions.

The fifteenth century saw the building of Ackergill Tower and Girnigoe Castle in Caithness, and also Balnagown Castle, the ancient seat of the Earls of Ross. The sixteenth century saw the building of Brims Castle, Keiss Castle and the Castle of Mey in Caithness, Castle Craig, the residence of the bishops of Ross, Cadboll Castle in Easter Ross and Ardvreck Castle on the shores of Loch Assynt where the gallant Montrose was imprisoned for a time after his defeat at Carbisdale. The seventeenth century produced Dunbeath Castle and Freswick House in Caithness, and Fairburn Tower and Kilcoy Castle in Ross and Cromarty. Many of these were seats of the clan chiefs and some remain so today. Erchless Castle is associated with the Clan Chisholm, Achnacarry with the Camerons, and Brahan Castle was the ancient seat of MacKenzie of Seaforth.

Many castles are still inhabited and cared for, examples being Ackergill Tower and Dunbeath Castle in Caithness while Castle Leod is still the seat of the Earl of Cromartie, and the Castle of Mey is the home of the Queen Mother. Not all castles are ancient, for Carbisdale in its spectacular setting overlooking the Kyle of Sutherland was built in the nineteenth century and is now used as a youth hostel. Many ancient castles have been restored, such as the small fifteenth-century Kinlochaline Castle situated at the head of Loch Aline. It was attacked and burned by Montrose's soldiers in 1644 and suffered damage by Cromwell's men, but was partially restored in the 1890s. Skibo Castle in Sutherland was bought by the millionaire Andrew Carnegie in 1898 and he spent £100,000 in restoring it for his Highland home.

The most impressive building on the east coast is Dunrobin Castle, built between 1846 and 1850 for the Duke and Duchess of Sutherland. It was designed by the architect Sir Charles Barry who also built the present Houses of Parliament. It has been compared with a château on the Loire, and the decor and furniture match the splendour of the outside. It was built around a much older castle and its massive inner keep dates from 1400.

Perhaps the most photographed of all Highland castles is Eilean Donan Castle in Wester Ross, occupying a tiny island at Dornie where Loch Duich and Loch Long meet Loch Alsh. It was for many years the stronghold of the MacKenzies of Kintail and was latterly occupied by the MacRaes. The original castle was a typical west Highland castle with a high curtain wall but in the fourteenth century a rectangular keep was built

at one corner. In 1331 Randolph, Earl of Moray, gave the wall
rather gruesome decorations—the heads of fifty victims. In
1719 it was the centre of the abortive Jacobite rising being held
by Spanish troops under the Earl of Seaforth, but was bom-
barded by three English men-of-war and blown up. Recon-
struction was carried out between 1912 and 1932 by the late
Col MacRae-Gilstrap and it now houses the clan MacRae war
memorial.

Many of the buildings listed in this section are open to the
public but many continue in use as private residences and must
be regarded as such by visitors.

MILITARY FORTS

As has been shown, the strategic importance of the Great Glen
had been recognised even in the thirteenth century and so it is
not surprising to find Cromwell busily building forts at Inverlochy and Inverness to control the region. The first fort at
Inverlochy, erected in 1654, was hastily constructed of turf and
wattle, then in 1690 King William of Orange sent General
MacKay with his soldiers to the Highlands. MacKay faced the
earthworks of Inverlochy with stones and re-named it Fort
William. In 1746 despite being besieged for the whole of the
rebellion Fort William was still holding out against the Jacobite
army.

The rebellions caused a spate of fort building; after 1715
emergency forts and garrison posts such as Bernera on the
Sound of Sleat and Kiliwhimin in the Great Glen were hastily
erected. In 1724 George I instructed General Wade to proceed
north and examine the state of the country. After his report
Fort George and Fort Augustus were built, both being much
superior architecturally to the earlier ones. Fort Augustus was
designed as the fortified residence of a governor with power of
command over all the forts and barracks in the Highlands and
the buildings still reveal today the intention of making it an

administrative centre as well as a barracks. Building began in 1729 and it was completed in 1742. In the '45 rebellion it fell after a two-day siege by the Jacobites, after a direct hit on a powder magazine from the old fort at Kiliwhimin half a mile away. It was retaken after Culloden and repairs were effected. In 1876 it was presented to the Benedictine Order for use as a monastery and in 1882 it was raised to the status of an abbey.

All that now remains of the old fort at Kiliwhimin is one wall standing in the backyard of the Lovat Arms Hotel, Fort Augustus. The fort at Fort William was garrisoned until 1860 but the only part still remaining is a section of the north-west ramparts and the governor's house.

CHURCHES

The first Christian missionary to Scotland was St Ninian who established a monastery at Whithorn about AD 400. Although his labours resulted in the conversion of the southern Picts there is no evidence to suspect that he penetrated the region north of the Great Glen, although one monk from Whithorn—St Duthus —is the patron saint of Tain. In AD 563 St Columba founded his monastery at Iona and it is known that he travelled as far north as Inverness in the territory of the northern Picts.

But more important in this region than either St Ninian or St Columba was St Maol Rubha who left his native Ireland in 671 and in 673 settled at Apurcrossan (now known as Applecross). He lived for some time on a small island in Loch Maree, founding a church there whose site is still visible.

There are numerous other known sites where early Celtic missionaries once preached the gospel. St Moluog founded the monastery at Fortrose in the sixth century and there were churches at Avoch, Arpafeelie and Rosemarkie.

The Celtic Church was gradually assimilated into the Roman Catholic Church and during the reign of Malcolm Canmore and David I the continental religious orders were first brought to Scotland. Canons Regular built the great abbey of Fearn near Tain in 1221, and in 1230 Valliscaulian monks built the priory at Beauly whose walls still stand.

Fearn Abbey has had a varied history. One of its most famous abbots, Patrick Hamilton, became a preacher of the Reformation and was burned at the stake at St Andrews in 1528. In 1724 the abbey was struck by lightning while a service was being held, the flagstone roof fell and thirty-eight people were killed. The abbey now restored is in use as the parish church of Fearn.

The post-Reformation churches are generally plain buildings reflecting the mood of the reformers and their dislike of ostentation, but some of them are of architectural interest, among them the church at Contin, and St Mary's Church, Lybster. The church and manse at Croick were among those designed by Thomas Telford in the early nineteenth century. This church has a sad tale associated with it from the time of the clearances. In 1845 a local laird evicted eighty-eight tenants from Glencalvie and they sought refuge in the churchyard, the minister not daring to let them take shelter in the church lest he should incur the wrath of the laird. For a week the people sheltered under their plaids in the churchyard before they made up their minds where they should go, and it is said that some marks on the diamond-paned windows were scratched by these poor people.

MEMORIALS

The old tradition of erecting a stone or pile of stones to commemorate a person or a deed still continues in the Highlands. More rarely an elaborate statue or monument is raised. One of the most gruesome monuments is the 'well of heads' beside Loch Oich. An inscription in English, Gaelic, French and Latin tells the story of how vengeance was ordered by Lord MacDonnel on the perpetrators of the foul murder of the Keppoch family. A father and his six sons were slain and their heads washed in the spring before being presented at the feet of the noble lord in Glengarry Castle.

The Jacobite rebellions brought a rich crop of memorials especially those on the battlefield of Culloden. The aftermath of the battle, too, is commemorated, for in Glen Moriston a cairn was erected in memory of one Roderick MacKenzie who bore a remarkable resemblance to Prince Charles. He was mistaken for the Prince and killed by troops engaged in the search. Prince Charles' point of departure from Loch nan Uamh is marked by a stone erected in 1956 by the Forty-Five Association.

All kinds of events are commemorated by memorials simple or elaborate. At Dornoch in a garden near the golf course stands a stone slab bearing the date 1722; it was here that the last witch in Scotland was burned to death. She was an old woman named Janet Horne who was found guilty of the ludicrous charge of transforming her daughter into a pony to ride to a witches' meeting. On a hilltop overlooking Evanton is the unusual Negapatam monument, a replica of the gates of this Indian city. It was set up by Sir Hector Munro of Novar in 1782 to commemorate his relief of the city in the Indian campaign. Between Drumnadrochit and Invermoriston a tall cairn stands in memory of John Cobb, the racing motorist, who lost his life when his speed-boat capsized on Loch Ness in September 1952 as he was attempting to break the water speed record.

The churchyards contain many interesting tombstones. The historic church of Balnakiel in Sutherland contains the grave of a noted robber and murderer Donald MacMurroch; it also contains the grave of the poet Rob Donn MacKay who died in 1788.

THE COUNTRYSIDE

Many institutions today encourage the enjoyment of the countryside to enable its recreational and educational potential to be exploited. The Countryside Commission for Scotland was set up in 1967 to advise the Secretary of State for Scotland on matters relating to the countryside. Among its functions it encourages local authorities to provide picnic sites, view points and visitor centres in the more interesting areas. The Forestry Commission too has provided in many of its forests such facilities as information centres, camping sites, forest walks and picnic places, while the Nature Conservancy has established nature reserves. The National Trust for Scotland preserves for the nation sites of historic interest as well as areas of great scenic beauty.

The Nature Reserves

The first national Nature Reserve in Britain was established by the Nature Conservancy in 1951 at Beinn Eighe in Ross and Cromarty, with the primary aim of preserving some of the few remaining fragments of Scotland's old pine forests at Coille na Glas Leitire (wood on the grey slope) along the southern shores of Loch Maree. The reserve's 10,507 acres cover deer forest country typical of north-west Scotland and include stretches of natural woodland and plantations of conifers, of moor and mountain, of lochans, bogs and streams. Animals on the reserve include pine marten, wild cat, otter, fox, red deer and roe deer, while birds include such rare species as the golden eagle and the peregrine falcon with ptarmigans on the mountain tops and red-throated and black-throated divers on Loch Maree.

There is a picnic site for visitors three miles from Kinlochewe which is the start of a nature trail through Glas Leitire. There are some beautiful stretches of forest but the trail also shows the effects of man's exploitation with the ruins of a furnace where iron was produced between 1607 and 1688.

Largest of all the reserves in the northern Highlands is Inverpolly which covers 26,827 acres of Ross and Cromarty, an area wild, remote and almost uninhabited, exhibiting a cross-section of Sutherland's scenery and taking in all of Loch Sionascaig with its birch-covered islands.

In 1962 an important extension was made to Inverpolly

reserve when the area around Knockan was added. Knockan cliff was the centre of a great scientific controversy in the mid-nineteenth century when geologists made a discovery that seemed to upset their most basic theories. Since 1815 it had been accepted that younger sedimentary rocks overlie older sediments and that the oldest are always most altered and reconstituted, but at Knockan the normal sequence is upset. The basal gneiss is followed by red sandstone, white quartzite and grey limestone in normal sequence but above this is highly altered mica schist forming the cliff itself and extending eastwards to build the mass of the mountains beyond.

It was not until 1884 that the controversy was settled when the existence of a great inclined thrust fault was proved. This has driven a huge wedge of older schist over the younger Cambrian sediments, a phenomenon which has now been recognised all over the world.

Another area of great geological interest is the 3,200-acre National Nature Reserve of Inchnadamph lying between Loch Assynt and Ben More Assynt, where the rare limestone fauna is protected by strict control of burning and grazing. Flowers here include globe flower, mountain avens, moss campion and purple saxifrage. This is typical limestone country where percolating rainwater has acted on the rock to form sink holes, underground streams and limestone caverns, the most famous being the caves of Allt nan Uamh where traces of early Stone Age man have been found with the remains of Pleistocene animals then native to Scotland.

At Allt nan Carnan Gorge to the north-west of Loch Carron a deep gully up to 80ft deep, its sides thickly wooded with oak, hazel, birch, ash, aspen, rowan and many more species, an area of 18 acres, has been set aside as a National Nature Reserve. About a mile north of the head of Loch Kishorn, Rassal ashwood, one of the few natural ashwoods in Scotland, has also been saved for the nation.

Other Nature Reserves include the one at Strathy Bog in

Sutherland, one of the best remaining examples of natural bog left in Scotland, and those at the Mound Alderwoods on the estuary of Loch Fleet, and at Invernaver near the mouth of the River Naver. Permission must be sought before visiting the last two and all Nature Reserves have rules that must be observed by visitors.

The National Trust for Scotland

The National Trust for Scotland was founded in 1931 to preserve places of natural beauty and of historic interest. It is a charity supported by the annual subscriptions of its members who numbered over 37,000 in 1972. It owns 7,000 acres of the Kyle–Plockton peninsula in Wester Ross, and 14,000 acres at Torridon with some of Scotland's finest mountain scenery. A famous beauty spot owned by the Trust is Corrieshalloch Gorge in Wester Ross where the Falls of Measach tumble 150ft into a mile-long gorge.

It has in its care the monument at Glenfinnan erected in memory of the clansmen who died in support of Prince Charles in 1745. An information centre here outlines the steps in the tragic campaign. It also cares for Hugh Miller's cottage at Cromarty, where visitors can see the rock specimens collected by that remarkable man.

At the end of a long sea-loch in Wester Ross surrounded by the barren hills of Torridon lies an oasis where exotic plants flourish, where lilies from the Himalayas and giant forget-me-nots from the South Pacific bloom in the shade of silver birch, Scots pine and palm trees. Yet in 1862 when Osgood MacKenzie set out to make his dream garden a reality the bare peninsula of Am Ploc Ard had only one dwarf willow growing.

When he died his daughter, Mrs Mairi Sawyer, carried on the work of tending and extending the garden and in 1952 to ensure its continuance she presented it to the National Trust for Scotland. Inverewe garden is open daily throughout the year and it attracts over 120,000 visitors each year.

212

There are many small towns in the northern Highlands, especially along the eastern coastal strip. This section deals only with some of the larger of them but the visitor should not overlook the numerous lesser towns and villages such as Ullapool, Lairg, Helmsdale, Golspie or Brora, or Plockton where the entire village is considered to be of great architectural interest.

Thurso

The town of Thurso is beautifully situated where the River Thurso enters a wide bay on the north coast of Caithness. Its harbour, like that of Scrabster nearby, is sheltered by the great cliffs of Holborn Head and Dunnet Head, while opposite lie the blue-grey hills of Hoy and the other isles of Orkney. In the Middle Ages Thurso was an important trading centre with ships sailing to the continent and in 1633 it was made a free burgh of barony.

The town shows clearly the three stages in its growth: along the harbour are old streets with fishermen's cottages dating from the seventeenth and eighteenth centuries—old houses built of brown and yellow sandstone their corners rounded by the wind that blows from the North Sea. The town centre shows the development that took place in the nineteenth century, while in the suburbs clusters of Scandinavian-style houses accommodate the workers who came from all parts of Britain to run the experimental fast reactor at Dounreay. This development caused a tremendous rise in Thurso's population from 3,249 in 1951 to 8,037 in 1961 so that Thurso has been called 'the boom town of the North'. It now has three primary schools, a new high school and a technical college.

The most interesting building is Old St Peter's Church whose churchyard has a tombstone dating from the fourteenth century.

213

It was in use until 1832. New St Peter's Church is a fine example of early nineteenth-century architecture and has recently been restored.

Wick

Although Wick was an important settlement in the time of the Norsemen and in 1503 became the seat of the Sheriff Court its greatest boost came in 1589 when it was made a Royal Burgh. It developed into an important trading centre and from 1589 to 1707 it sent its own commissioners to the Scottish parliament.

Thanks to the efforts of Sir John Sinclair, a proper harbour was constructed by Thomas Telford and named Pulteneytown after the chairman of the Fisheries Commission, Sir William Pulteney. It was completed in 1810 but the herring industry developed so rapidly that in 1824 the building of an outer harbour began. By 1862 1,122 boats were operating from Wick during the summer herring season, and work was available for thousands of shore workers in curing herring, making barrels and keeping boats and sails in good order. The herring industry declined rapidly after the turn of the century to be replaced by the smaller white fish industry which received a boost with the introduction of the seine net in the 1920s. Wick still has a fishing fleet and ice plant, and engineering shops play their part, but the great herring boom has gone—probably for ever.

There are several new industries in Wick, one of the most interesting being glass blowing which started in 1959 through the efforts of a local landowner concerned at the unemployment that followed the end of construction work at Dounreay. The factory now attracts more than 50,000 visitors a year. Other small enterprises include a laundry and a recording studio that has produced some remarkably good records, many of them featuring the Wick Scottish Dance Band. There is a distillery at Pulteneytown with an output of 8,000gal a week, most of which is sent south for blending although a little is retained and sold as Old Pulteney.

Wick's population has remained remarkably steady. From its peak population of 8,674 in 1911 it declined to 7,161 in 1951 but it had risen to 7,418 in 1966.

Dornoch

Dornoch is one of the most delightful towns in Scotland. It is a tiny place with a population of under one thousand yet it has a long and fascinating history, its first charter dating back to 1275. The old houses of yellow sandstone give the town a quiet medieval flavour and the cathedral in the centre enhances its appearance and adds dignity.

The cathedral was begun in 1222 by Gilbert de Moravia, bishop of Caithness, and is modelled on Elgin cathedral which was in turn modelled on the great cathedral of Lincoln. It was destroyed by fire in 1570 during a clan feud between the Murrays of Dornoch and the MacKays of Strathnaver and only the tower and steeple were left standing. In 1616 the choir and transept were restored by Sir Robert Gordon, the nave was restored in 1634 and between 1835 and 1837 Countess Elizabeth, the dowager Duchess of Sutherland had the whole building renovated, many stained glass windows replaced, and the church furnished in carved oak.

Dornoch Castle, opposite the cathedral, was originally the bishop's palace. It too was ravaged by fire in 1570 only one tower surviving. Since then it has been successively the residence of Sir Robert Gordon, the tolbooth, the county court house, the prison and is now a hotel.

Today Dornoch is primarily a tourist centre taking advantage of its rich history, its marvellous sandy beach and its golf course where the game has been played since 1616.

Tain

Tain is another ancient town, its patron saint St Duthus

being born here in the sixth century. He built a chapel and as was commonly done in medieval times a sanctuary was established round the church, its limits marked by four corner crosses, inside which the law of the church would protect a fugitive against arrest or violence. Robert the Bruce sent his queen and her ladies here for safety, but the sanctuary was violated by the Earl of Ross who handed them over to the English.

In 1066 Malcolm Canmore granted the town certain trading privileges and the town today is justly proud of its 900 years of history. St Duthus Memorial Church was founded in the fifteenth century. In 1487 at the instigation of James VI it was erected into a collegiate church with a provost, five canons, two deacons, a sacrist and three singing boys thus consolidating Tain's position as one of the most important religious centres of the north of Scotland.

In the sixteenth century Tain grew as a trading centre exporting skins, hides and salmon as well as iron produced from bog iron ore near Edderton. But by the end of the seventeenth century Tain had suffered a recession, many of the buildings were decaying and the town's tolbooth and steeple being in a ruinous condition had to be demolished. A new tolbooth and steeple were built between 1706 and 1733, and this is now one of Tain's most distinctive buildings. Its tower is square and solid-looking, topped by five fat pinnacles and a spire. Below it stands the town's ancient mercat cross.

Today Tain is best known as a holiday centre and as a market town but its population is expected to increase by between 10,000 and 20,000 on account of oil-related developments in the Cromarty Firth area.

Dingwall

Dingwall derived its name from the Norse 'thing vollr' (place of the law court) thus indicating a certain importance even in those days. It became a Royal Burgh in 1226 its charter granted by King Alexander II. Only a fragment of the old royal castle, the seat of the Earls of Ross, is still standing but this was the scene of an abortive plot between the last earl and the Douglas to divide Scotland between them.

The Town House with its distinctive steeple was built in 1730 and outside can be seen the shaft of the old mercat cross and the old iron yett (gate) of the former gaol.

Dingwall cherishes its connection with Sir Hector MacDonald, the crofter's son who rose from private to major-general commanding the Highland Brigade. He paid a visit to the town after his triumph at Omdurman and is commemorated by a tower on the hill south of the town. The sword presented to him by the Clan Donald is preserved in the council chambers as is the one he wore as an aide-de-camp to Queen Victoria.

The new A9 will by-pass the town and planners have decided that the main street will be 'pedestrianised'. It is unlikely that Dingwall will suffer the impact of industrialisation as much as Tain and other parts of Easter Ross, but it will certainly grow as an administrative centre and a shopping centre.

Fortrose

On either side of a promontory of yellow sand lie the two parts of the burgh of Fortrose—Fortrose itself and Rosemarkie. Rosemarkie is by far the oldest, a Culdee monastery being founded here in the sixth century by St Moluog. The saint most closely associated with Rosemarkie, however, is St Boniface who also built a church here. A relic of Pictish days is the sculptured stone that stands in the churchyard and which, it is believed, may mark the grave of St Moluog.

Rosemarkie became a Royal Burgh in 1216 but about 1240 when Chanonry (the old name for Fortrose) was chosen as the site of the cathedral of Ross, the old town lost some of its importance. In 1455 it was joined to Chanonry by James II and the two towns became the Royal Burgh of Fortrose.

Most magnificent of all antiquities in the Black Isle is Fortrose

Cathedral, a red sandstone building which was 192ft long but of which only the south aisle of the nave remains. Even this is sufficient to show how splendid the whole cathedral must have been.

INDUSTRIAL ARCHAEOLOGY

The absence of large-scale industrial developments has long been a feature of the Highlands. There are the relics, already mentioned, of iron smelting near Loch Maree and at Strontian there are traces of the old lead mines, furnaces, wagonways and houses established in the early seventeenth century. The old quarries at Castletown and Lybster are reminders of the great flagstone industry of the nineteenth century in Caithness. The town of Brora is unique in the northern Highlands because Jurassic coal has been worked here since the sixteenth century, an activity which in the eighteenth century led to the development of salt production and brick making. An engineering shop was established at Brora by the Duke of Sutherland in 1871 while work was proceeding on the Golspie to Helmsdale railway line. The shop produced only one locomotive and is now used as a tweed mill.

The history of legal distilling goes back to the early nineteenth century. Edderton distillery was founded in 1800; part of Teaninich distillery at Alness dates from 1840 and Glenmorangie distillery near Tain was founded in 1843. As has been mentioned earlier, at Spinningdale there are the remains of the cotton mill established by George MacIntosh and David Dale.

There are numerous relics from the early days of the fishing industry with tiny harbours all along the east coast. Keiss has a delightful little harbour and some old houses survive built of local sandstone and roofed with slate. Cromarty harbour was built by the local laird George Ross in 1785 and the original harbour at Avoch was laid out by Telford between 1813 and 1815. On the west coast Ullapool was built between 1788 and 1796 as a planned village laid out on a grid system. The tiny harbour at Whaligoe was once the scene of much activity with boats discharging their catches while women climbed the 365 steps with baskets of herring on their backs.

There are relics too of the long struggle to wrest a living from the land. Several water mills have survived in Caithness, and Old Millnain Mill near Strathpeffer is being converted into bed and breakfast accommodation and a small museum. A thatched croft house at Laidhay north of Dunbeath in Caithness has been converted into a folk museum by the Laidhay Preservation Trust set up in 1960.

The old croft houses of last century were replaced by stone-built buildings of two storeys, their walls often white-washed or painted. They generally have two large rooms on the ground floor with a scullery at the back while a narrow staircase leads to three small bedrooms under the slate roof lit by dormer windows. Today new croft houses are generally bungalows and local stone is hardly ever used. The buildings are of concrete block construction, harled outside and roofed with concrete tiles or ruberoid slates. There are still many ruined cottages standing as sad and silent reminders of the clearances of the nineteenth century.

As interesting are the remains that show the development of communication. The routes followed by early cattle drovers are still useful to those who seek the remote parts and the roads of Wade, Caulfield and Telford are now surfaced with tarmacadam, while some of Telford's bridges are still in use. The railways to Mallaig, Kyle of Lochalsh and Thurso still retain their attraction for visitors and there are traces of a still more extensive network such as the Wick to Lybster Light Railway. The great viaducts at Loch nan Uamh, Glenfinnan and Morar remain a tribute to the pioneers who built them. The Caledonian canal with its sea basins and locks is another tribute to the great engineer Telford and it is likely that this marvellous highway will soon realise its full potential as a tourist attraction.

Along the coast the lighthouses show the steady progress in

making sea routes safe, Cape Wrath lighthouse dating from 1828, that of Ardnamurchan from 1848 while the newest of them all, that at Strathy Point, was commissioned in 1958.

Industrial projects since World War II have generally been carried out with the aim of blending as far as possible with their surroundings, the facing of hydro-electric dams and power stations with local stone being an example of this imaginative approach. In the same way although the sphere of the experimental fast reactor at Dounreay is huge it is somehow dwarfed by the sheer size of the plain of Caithness. Largest of all are the yards building oil production platforms, and what they will look like in 100 years is difficult to predict. Today emphasis is placed on the importance of restoring these sites to their former state. This will please conservationists but may rob the industrial archaeologist of much fascinating material.

Many relics of the past are carefully preserved in museums at Inverness and Fort William, the latter having a marvellous collection of Jacobite relics. Smaller museums are important too, that of Thurso covering the entire range of local industry; one of its most interesting displays is a simulated room with open fire, wooden furniture and china crockery and ornaments —a typical nineteenth-century home.

BIBLIOGRAPHY

Adam, F. *The Clans, Septs and Regiments of the Scottish Highlands,*
eighth edition, revised by Sir Thomas Innes of Learney (1970)
Agriculture & Fisheries for Scotland, Department of. *Land Use in
the Highlands & Islands* (HMSO Edinburgh, 1964)
———. *Regulation of Scottish Inshore Fisheries,* Report of the Scottish
Inshore Fisheries Committee (HMSO Edinburgh, 1970)
———. *Report of the Commission of Enquiry into Crofting Conditions*
(HMSO Edinburgh, 1954)
———. *Scottish Peat Surveys,* Vol 4 (HMSO Edinburgh, 1968)
———. *Scottish Sea Fisheries Statistical Tables, 1972* (HMSO Edin-
burgh, 1973)
Air Ministry. *Climatological Atlas of the British Isles* (HMSO 1952)
An Comunn Gaidhealach, Inverness; pamphlets
Anson, P. F. *Scots Fisherfolk* (Banff, 1950)
Baynes, J. *The Jacobite Rising of 1715* (1970)
Butt, J. *Industrial Archaeology of Scotland* (Newton Abbot, 1967)
Campbell, G. *Highland Heritage* (1962)
Collier, A. *The Crofting Problem* (1953)
Collinson, F. *The Traditional and National Music of Scotland* (1966)
Craig, G. Y. (ed). *The Geology of Scotland,* new edition (1970)
Crofters, Commission, Annual Reports (in progress)
Cruden, S. *Scottish Abbeys* (HMSO Edinburgh, 1960)
———. *The Early Christian and Pictish Monuments of Scotland,* Ministry
of Works Illustrated Guide Book (HMSO Edinburgh, 1964)
———. *The Scottish Castle* (1960)
Daiches, D. *Scotch Whisky* (1969)
Darling, F. Fraser. *A Herd of Red Deer* (1937)
———. *Crofting Agriculture* (Edinburgh and London, 1945)
———. *Natural History in the Highlands & Islands* (1947)
———. *West Highland Survey* (1955)
Darling, F. Fraser and Boyd, J. M. *The Highlands & Islands* (1964)

221

BIBLIOGRAPHY

Dickinson, W. C.   *Scotland From the Earliest Times to 1603*, A New History of Scotland, Vol 1 (Edinburgh and London, 1961)

Dinsdale, T.   *Loch Ness Monster* (1961)

Donaldson, G.   *Northwards by Sea* (Edinburgh, 1966)

Fresson, E. E.   *Air Road to the Isles* (1967)

Geddes, T.   *Hebridean Sharker* (1960)

Geikie, A.   *The Scenery of Scotland* (1865)

Geological Sciences, Institute of.   *A Summary of the Mineral Resources of the 'Crofter Counties' of Scotland* (HMSO 1969)

Glasgow School of Art.   *Gairloch–Poolewe: Tir na Mara*, Planning Project No 1: Wester Ross (Scottish Tourist Board, 1967)

Grant, D.   *Old Thurso*, Caithness Notebooks, No 4 (Thurso, 1966)

Gray, M.   'Crofting and Fishing in the North West Highlands 1890–1914', *Northern Scotland*, Vol 1 No 1, December, 1972 (Centre for Scottish Studies, University of Aberdeen)

Grimble, I.   *The Trial of Patrick Sellar* (1962)

———.   *Chief of MacKay* (1965)

Gunn, N.   *Morning Tide* (1931)

———.   *The Lost Glen* (1932)

———.   *Butcher's Broom* (1934)

———.   *The Silver Darlings* (1941)

———.   *The Green Isle of the Great Deep* (1944)

———.   *The Atom of Delight* (1956)

Haldane, A. R. B.   *The Drove Roads of Scotland* (Edinburgh, 1952)

———.   *New Ways Through the Glens* (Edinburgh, 1962)

———.   *Three Centuries of Scottish Posts* (Edinburgh, 1971)

Harris, R. A. and Duff, K. R.   *Wild Deer in Britain* (Newton Abbot, 1970)

Harvie-Brown, J. A. and Buckley, T. E.   *A Vertebrate Fauna of Sutherland, Caithness & West Cromarty* (Edinburgh, 1887)

Henderson, I.   *The Picts* (1967)

Highlands & Islands Development Board.   *Explore the Highlands & Islands* (Inverness, undated)

———.   *Strath of Kildonan*, Special Report No 5 (Inverness, 1970)

———.   Annual Reports (in progress)

Jack Holmes Planning Group, The.   *The Moray Firth*, A plan for growth in a sub-region of the Scottish Highlands; A report to the HIDB 1968

Kermack, W. R.   *The Scottish Highlands* (Edinburgh, 1957)

Kyd, J. G. (ed).   *Scottish Population Statistics* (Edinburgh, 1952)

Lacaille, A. D.   *The Stone Age in Scotland* (1954)

Linklater, E.   *The Prince in the Heather* (1965)

MacBrayne, D. Limited.   *A Hundred Years of Progress*, MacBrayne centenary 1851–1951 (Glasgow, 1951)

MacCulloch, D. B.   *Romantic Lochaber*, Third edition (Edinburgh, 1971)

McDowell, R. J. S.   *The Whiskies of Scotland* (1967)

MacKenzie, A.   *The Prophecies of the Brahan Seer* (Stirling, 1899; New edition Golspie, 1970)

McKenzie, O.   *A Hundred Years in the Highlands* (1924)

McKenzie, W. C.   *A Short History of Scotland* (Paisley, 1906)

Mackie, A.   *Scottish Pageantry* (1967)

McNally, L.   *Highland Year* (1967)

McVean, D. N. and Ratcliffe, D. A.   *Plant Communities of the Scottish Highlands* (HMSO 1962)

Marshall, E.   *The Black Isle. A Portrait of the Past* (Dingwall, 1973)

Maxwell, G.   *Harpoon at a Venture* (1952)

——.   *Ring of Bright Water* (1960)

——.   *The Rocks Remain* (1963)

——.   *Raven Seek Thy Brother* (1968)

Meteorological Office.   *Tables of Temperature, Relative Humidity, Precipitation and Sunshine for the World*, Part 3; Europe and the Azores (HMSO 1972)

Miller, H.   *My Schools and Schoolmasters* (Edinburgh, 1854)

——.   *The Old Red Sandstone* (Edinburgh, 1841)

Mitchell, J.   *Reminiscences of My Life in the Highlands* (1884, republished Newton Abbot, 1970)

Mitchison, R.   *Agricultural Sir John* (1962)

Munro, J. and Taylor, I. C.   *Glenfinnan and the '45* (National Trust for Scotland, Edinburgh, undated)

Munro, R. W. and Munro, J.   *Tain Through the Centuries* (Tain, 1966)

Napier Commission.   *Evidence Taken by HM Commissioners of Inquiry into the Conditions of the Crofters and Cottars in the Highlands & Islands of Scotland* (Edinburgh, 1884)

Nethersole Thompson, D.   *Highland Birds* (Inverness, 1971)

O'Dell, A. C. and Walton, K.   *The Highlands & Islands of Scotland* (1960)

Omand, D. (ed).   *The Caithness Book* (Inverness, 1972)

Phemister, J.   *British Regional Geology Scotland: The Northern Highlands*, second edition (HMSO Edinburgh, 1948)

Piggott, S. (ed).   *The Prehistoric Peoples of Scotland* (1962)

BIBLIOGRAPHY

Pine, L. G. *The Highland Clans* (Newton Abbot, 1972)
Poucher, W. A. *The Scottish Peaks* (1968)
Prebble, J. *Culloden* (1961)
——. *The Highland Clearances* (1963)
Pryde, G. S. *Scotland From 1603 to the Present Day*, A New History of Scotland, Vol 2 (Edinburgh and London, 1961)
Robertson, B. *Jacobite Activities In and Around Inverness, 1688–1746* (Blairgowrie, 1970)
Ross, J. *Whisky* (1970)
Saxon, J. *The Fossil Fishes of Caithness and Orkney*, Caithness Notebooks No 6 (Thurso, 1967)
Scottish Office. *Scottish Abstract of Statistics No 2/1972* (HMSO 1973)
Senior, W. H. and Swan, W. B. *The Report of a Survey of Agriculture in Caithness, Orkney and Shetland* (HIDB Inverness, 1972)
Sinclair, C. *The Thatched Houses of the Old Highlands* (Edinburgh, 1953)
Sinclair, Sir J. (ed). *The Statistical Account of Scotland 1791–1799* (Edinburgh, undated)
Smith, I. C. *Consider the Lilies* (1968)
Smout, T. C. *A History of the Scottish People 1560–1830* (1969)
Steven, H. M. and Carlisle, A. *The Native Pinewoods of Scotland* (Edinburgh, 1959)
Stewart, Col D. *Sketches of the Character, Manners and Present State of the Highlanders of Scotland*, two volumes (Edinburgh, 1822)
Swire, O. F. *The Highlands and Their Legends* (Edinburgh, 1963)
Taylor, Lt-Col I. B. C. *The Story of Tartan*, An Comunn Gaidhealach Pamphlet No 7 (Inverness, 1967)
Thom, A. *Megalithic Lunar Observatories* (1971)
Thomas, J. *The West Highland Railway* (Newton Abbot, 1965)
Thomson, D. C. and Grimble, I. (eds). *The Future of the Highlands* (1968)
Tranter, N. *The Fortified House in Scotland*, Vol 5 (Edinburgh, 1966)
Vallance, H. A. *The Highland Railway* (Newton Abbot, 1969)
Vining, E. G. *Flora MacDonald* (1967)
Wainwright, F. T. (ed). *The Problem of the Picts* (Edinburgh, 1955)
—— (ed). *The Northern Isles* (1962)
Waterston, C. D. *Hugh Miller* (National Trust for Scotland, Edinburgh, undated)
Weir, T. *Scottish Lochs*, two volumes (1970, 1972)

West, T. W.   *A History of Architecture in Scotland* (1967)
Whitehead, G. K.   *The Wild Goats of Great Britain and Ireland* (Newton Abbot, 1972)
Young, D.   *Scotland* (1971)

ACKNOWLEDGEMENTS

I WISH to thank the many people who provided information for this book. The list includes Mr Colin Spencer, Comhordanaiche, An Comunn Gaidhealach; Mr D. J. Watkins, West Highland School of Adventure; Miss Anne Burgess, Area Tourist Officer, Wester Ross Tourist Organisation; Dr Futty of the MacAulay Institute for Soil Research; Mr E. E. Pritchard, Brora; Mr T. M. Hunter, Brora; Mr Grant, Regional Director, North of Scotland College of Agriculture; Mr Campbell McLachlan of the British Deer Society; Mr Campbell, Regional Officer, West Scotland Nature Conservancy Council; the Managing Director of Messrs MacRae & Dick, Inverness; and the Information Officers of Dounreay Atomic Energy Establishment, the Invergordon Distillers Group, the British Aluminium Co Ltd, and Wiggins Teape Ltd, Fort William mill.

The officials of many government and local government offices went to much trouble on my behalf. I am indebted to the staff of the Crofters, Commission, the Forestry Commission, the Highlands and Islands Development Board, and the County Clerks and County Surveyors of Caithness, Sutherland, Ross and Cromarty and Inverness-shire, while the Planning Officer of Inverness-shire provided some valuable material.

Most of all I am indebted to Mr D. J. MacRitchie, the HIDB's representative in Shetland. Mr MacRitchie read my manuscript and provided much additional information.

INDEX

Page references in italic indicate illustrations

INDEX

INDEX